This book is dedicated to Neil, Sam and Sammy

Lemonade FOR THE Lawnboy

THE EXECUTIVES' WIVES' COOKBOOK COMMITTEE

DAVID W. COOK II

JANET LETNES MARTIN

ILLUSTRATED BY DAVID W. COOK II

Martin House Publications

Martin House Publications
Box 274
Hastings, MN 55033

Copyright 2007
by David W. Cook II
and Janet Letnes Martin

Printed in the United States of America
Published by Martin House Publications
PO Box 274, Hastings, MN 55033

ISBN 1-886627-14-2

First Edition

Cover Illustration: David W. Cook II
Edited by: Jennifer L. Cook and Margaret Goderstad
Graphic Designer: Beth VanDeWalker
Printed by: Sentinel Printing St. Cloud, MN

✳

CONTENTS

PART I: THE COMMITTEE

The Executives' Wives' Cookbook Committee 2

Mrs. Jonathan Hurlinger 4

Beebe Hall 6

Mrs. Elmer Steele 8

Mrs. Charles Chatterton 10

Mrs. Stanley Bigsbee 14

Mrs. Molly McCurdle 16

Mrs. Grant Goldman-Hues 20

Mrs. Samuel Squire 24

Mrs. Michael Stellar 28

Mrs. E.O. Bittleduke 32

Katrina Canfield 36

Martha Payne 38

Mrs. Christina Pebbleworth-Stafford 40

Bunny Baxley 42

Doris Dupré 44

Maribelle Biche 48

PART II: THE COOKBOOK

Mrs. Jonathan Hurlinger 52

Beebe Hall 58

Mrs. Elmer Steele 70

Mrs. Charles Chatterton 76

Mrs. Stanley Bigsbee 80

Mrs. Molly McCurdle 86

Mrs. Grant Goldman-Hues 92

Mrs. Samuel Squire 96

Mrs. Michael Stellar 102

Mrs. E.O. Bittleduke 108

Katrina Canfield 114

Martha Payne 120

Mrs. Christina Pebbleworth-Stafford 124

Bunny Baxley 130

Doris Dupré 140

Maribelle Biche 148

PART III: THE LADIES AND THEIR CHARITY BALLS

The La La La La Lipstick Ball 157

The Butterfly Ball 158

The Masquerade Ball 160

The Executives' Wives' Cookbook Committee 162

PREFACE

It can be said that every **book** has a **story**, and every **story** could be a **book**. That said, this book contains the stories (and the recipes) of sixteen "upper crust" ladies who joined together to form The Executives' Wives' Cookbook Committee for the purpose of raising funds for charitable causes. However, the stories about these ladies and their lives are what make this book a different story in itself! And the stories behind the creators of this book are stories that could become several other books. We will begin telling the story behind the creators of this book.

David W. Cook

David W. Cook, a successful and celebrated artist who grew up in Minnetonka, Minnesota has been painting "my ladies", as he calls them, for over twenty years. He has studied, observed, and sometimes catered for "his ladies" in Chicago, Los Angeles, New York, and other places he has called home. In addition to cultivating "his ladies", David is a noted painter and sculptor whose works have been shown in many galleries and museums. His memories of being The Lawnboy to "these ladies" are vivid, and his childhood tales are woven throughout this book.

Janet Letnes Martin

Janet Letnes Martin, a native of Hillsboro, North Dakota, graduate of Augsburg College, and a 37-year resident of Hastings, Minnesota, is an author, publisher and speaker who has co-authored 16 books. One of her books, Growing Up Lutheran: What does this mean?, co-authored with Suzann Nelson, won the coveted Minnesota Book Award for Humor, and was produced into a musical comedy entitled Church Basement Ladies. This wildly successful musical has been playing to a full house for over two years in Minneapolis, Minnesota, and is mounting a national tour. This mother of three daughters, Jennifer, Sarah and Katrina and two sons-in-law Steve and Andy and grandmother of three wonderful little girls, Sophia, Ariana and Myana, has been writing and speaking about "the lighter side of life" for over twenty years.

These two artists/creators met and combined their talents to produce this book which had been a dream and vision of David Cook's for over twenty years. David grew up eating Châteaubriand, Bouef Bourguignon and Crème de Menthe sundaes prepared by his mother whose bible was *Bon Appétit*. Janet has co-authored two cookbooks, Lutheran Church Basement Women and Our Beloved Sweden-cookbooks that document immigrant and church basement food.

The recipe for this book is a winner! By combining David's marvelous paintings with David and Janet's witty and sometimes sarcastic humor, this book not only documents a time in history when Julia Child and Jackie Kennedy brought excitement and nouvelle cuisine to America's kitchens, but also tells the stories of "the ladies" whose lives revolved around themselves, their cash, their country club, their clothes, their conditions, their Cadillacs, the click of their compacts, and of course, their right-hand man and handsome hero, The Lawnboy.

David and Janet have thoroughly enjoyed collaborating on this project, and they couldn't have done it without all the help and encouragement of their families and friends. David dedicates this book to his nephew, Sam, who "gets it", and to his beloved dog, Sammy.

Janet dedicates this book to her late husband, Neil, who "kept her grounded"; and whom she misses dearly.

They want to especially thank their editors, Jennifer L. Cook and Margaret Goderstad, graphic designer Beth Van deWalker, their mutual friends, the Hildebrandts, and Janet's sister Nancy Edison.

lemonade.

PART I

THE COMMITTEE

THE EXECUTIVES' WIVES' COOKBOOK COMMITTEE

The idea to publish a cookbook to raise funds for worthy causes was the brainchild of Mrs. Elmer Steele. She single-handedly sent out invitations to 150 capable, bright ladies inviting them to a kick-off luncheon to come on board, and to see her dream come to fulfillment. Much to her embarrassment, only sixteen ladies showed up, but these sixteen appeared committed, enthusiastic and seemingly ready to work; even though they were pre-warned in the invitations that it would be an exhausting, monumental undertaking.

She opened the luncheon by telling the ladies that publishing a cookbook to be written by executives' wives for worthy causes was her idea; the work, satisfaction, and glory would be shared by all of them. She said she would be more than honored to be the President of The Executives' Wives' Cookbook Committee, but to be fair, they would all have the opportunity to cast a secret ballot for the purpose of letting everyone choose whom they thought would be the most capable president of this honorable committee.

Before the vote, both Bunny Baxley and Beebe Hall made it clear that they didn't want to be president, but they sure would help with the parties and the balls. By the way they were slurring their words everyone knew that Mrs. Charles Chatterton and Mrs. Stanley Bigsbee wouldn't be the smartest choices, so they unknowingly eliminated themselves.

Mrs. Molly McCurdle, in her enthusiastic way, said she would give everything she could to see the cookbook become a reality, but she couldn't be president because her daughters' ballet and piano lessons, and social graces classes were her first priorities.

Both Doris Dupré and Martha Payne said they didn't want to be president, and neither of them offered an explanation. Mrs. E.O. Bittleduke told everyone that her husband's condition made it impossible for her to be president, but she would help as much as she could. Mrs. Samuel

Squire, Mrs. Michael Stellar, and Mrs. Grant Goldman-Hues all said their social calendars prevented them from undertaking the obligation of the presidency, but they would be more than willing to help in whatever capacity needed whenever they were in town.

So the list of viable candidates for President of The Executives' Wives' Cookbook Committee came down to five ladies: Katrina Canfield, Mrs. Christina Pebbleworth-Stafford, Mrs. Jonathan Hurlinger, Maribelle Biche and Mrs. Elmer Steele.

The secret ballots were cast, the votes were tallied, and Mrs. Elmer Steele, much to her chagrin and horror, was not chosen to be the president. However, being the pillar of steel that she has always been known to be, handled the humiliation with the

2

utmost of strength, and graciously offered to help the newly chosen president, Mrs. Jonathan Hurlinger; even though it just about did her in to think about having to turn over the baton and the tiara.

It came as no surprise to the other ladies that Mrs. Jonathan Hurlinger was chosen. It was a no-brainer for those who weren't running for president. All the ladies that were involved in the voting had been on some committee with Mrs. Elmer Steele at the helm, and they knew first-hand that it was nearly impossible to work under her. As a matter of fact, she only received two votes. Most of the ladies knew she probably voted for herself, and the other vote was most likely from Martha Payne.

Secretly, both Katrina Canfield and Mrs. Christina Pebbleworth-Stafford wanted to be elected president in the worst way, but it was their 'attitudes' that eliminated them, and even they knew it. Each of them received only one vote, and everyone knew each voted for herself.

Everyone was puzzled that Maribelle Biche would even consider running, as mean as she was to everyone. She didn't get any votes, not even her own.

So, it came down to Mrs. Jonathan Hurlinger. She was their president. As a matter of fact, *she was no mere person, but something else entirely!*

Post Script: Deep down Mrs. Jonathan Hurlinger was confident she would be chosen president. She believed, as she had told her husband many times, "Of course, I do everything in the best and brightest way. After all, I was voted most likely to succeed in high school."

After voting, lunch, and many martinis, Mrs. Jonathan Hurlinger, with gavel in hand, took over the helm. She was very emotional, and appeared genuinely touched as she thanked the committee for putting its confidence in her. She, being the organized, capable person that the committee elected, immediately invited them all to the kick-

off dinner that she said she would be hosting within two weeks. She promised to have their committee assignments ready by the time of the kick-off dinner and thanked them again.

Even though she had rehearsed her acceptance speech before she was elected, she wasn't as totally in control as she thought she would be. As a matter of fact, she sat down and unashamedly cried uncontrollably, either from the realization of what had just happened, or from all the martinis she had consumed.

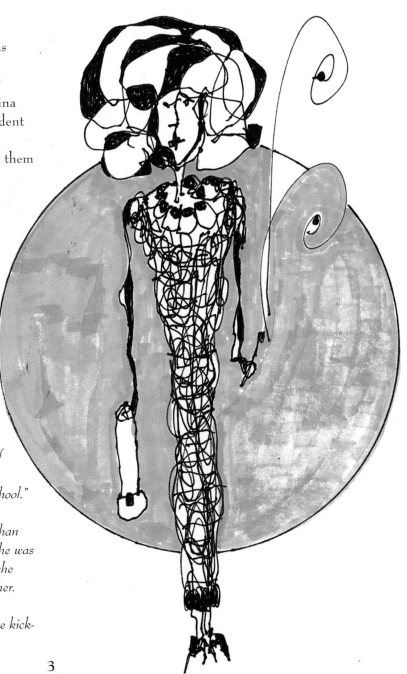

MRS. JONATHAN HURLINGER

MRS. JONATHAN HURLINGER

Anyone who has ever been privileged to be in the company of, or better yet, an intimate personal friend of Mrs. Jonathan Hurlinger, knows she is no mere person, but something else entirely.

Her distinct family structure is legendary. It is a well known fact that her husband, Jonathan, a successful lawyer of style, was totally smitten by not only her family structure, but also her many passions; especially her passions of indulging in the fine art of entertaining, and her visionary passion of pursuing and understanding both European and American culinary arts.

Mrs. Jonathan Hurlinger recently donated her elegantly, decorated kitchen and her precious time to research recipes with her favorite French chef, Pierre.[1] She took on this monumental task because, as President of The Executives' Wives' Cookbook Committee, she was, as she always is, committed to the cause, and only the best will do.

If that was not enough, the same week she threw a grand and most elegant birthday party for her dear friend, Mrs. Charles Chatterton. Her devotion to details was unsurpassed, down to party favors of French crystal martini glasses etched with Mrs. Charles Chatterton's favorite martini recipe. Her brilliance and creativity is quite amazing. It is no wonder she was chosen President of The Executives' Wives' Cookbook Committee.

It is refreshing to watch the Hurlingers and their compassionate devotion not only to their friends and community, but also to each other. This capable lady, brilliantly and with endearing charm, mimics her husband, and entertains his clients with the utmost of sophisticated humor and style. He, as a most successful lawyer, is able to more than amply provide all that is needed for her to pursue her many-faceted passions. They are truly the envy of all their friends.

MRS. JONATHAN HURLINGER'S THIRST-QUENCHING RECIPE FOR THE LAWNBOY

1 cup water
1 cup white sugar
5 ounces of reconstituted lemon juice
1 large lemon
1 ¾ cups ice water

Combine the water and sugar in a saucepan and bring to a boil. Stir constantly until the sugar is completely dissolved. Chill for 3 to 4 hours. Pour the mixture and the ice water into a tall pitcher and add the lemon juice. Cut the lemon into thin wedges and put them in a pitcher. Stir the mixture and pour it into chilled glasses. Add ice to each glass.

Everything about Mrs. Jonathan Hurlinger was about 'being lovely'- including her lawn. When The Lawnboy, (who was always warmly greeted by Mrs. Jonathan Hurlinger with "Oh, darling, my nails are still drying; I'm glad you're here; make it beautiful") came to mow on the day she hosted her annual, ladies' martini luncheon, he knew how important it was to please her, and he didn't let her down.

Even though she had many important tasks to tend to on the day she was hosting The Executives' Wives' Cookbook Committee, she made sure she didn't forget to serve lemonade to The Lawnboy; and she always served it to him in a large, fancy glass.

---

[1] *Pierre, the supposedly well-known French chef that she hired, is not only temperamental and eccentric, but this short-in-stature recluse has never told anyone any information about himself, including his last name. It is rumored he is a not-so-distant relative of André Michelin, and that means everything to Mrs. Jonathan Hurlinger.*

BEEBE HALL

BEEBE HALL

Beebe Hall could be described as an artist who had a flair for fashion, fire and French flambé! Why, she is something else! Her friend, Bunny, called her 'a ball of fire.' Others have characterized her as a lady with a savvy sense of style, a razor sharp wit and a strange obsession with fire.

Beebe was an only child born to two, privileged, intellectual, rather bizarre people. Her father was a noted and well-respected Scottish paleontologist whose passion and obsession was to locate the Loch Ness Monster. Her eccentric mother, whose lineage could be traced back to Louis XVI, was a pyrotechnics/pyromaniac genius and a well-known arsonist. Beebe took after her mother.[2]

Because of her father's work and his obsession with finding the monster, the family spent summers on the shores of Loch Ness. Beebe's mother, whose passions and interests were in fire, spent her time with Beebe at her side, making pyro on the shores of Loch Ness.

Every summer, Beebe and her mom would leave her father at the Ness during July and follow the fireworks from the Potomac to Paris, and conclude their holiday with attending 'Burning Viking Ship' festivals held in and around Inverness, Scotland. When Beebe was older, she was sent to summer camp to learn things and occupy her time. Without fail, she always became best buddies with the counselor who was in charge of bonfires and final night fireworks.

After she married Jimmy Hall, a successful CEO of his own insurance company, she tried to humor him and keep the flames alive by saying, "Home Is Where the Hearth Is." However, as Beebe told the 'couch man' who her husband, Jimmy, insisted she go see after she had burned down their garden shed and nearly burned down their house; "Why would you expect me to act any differently? It's what I know, what I like, and who I am."

The ladies of The Executives' Wives' Cookbook Committee knew Beebe Hall, who always smelled of smoke, was a tad bit touched by fire. They all agreed Beebe Hall needed to be included in a cookbook committee because no one else's flambe' recipes could hold a match to hers, and if you have that kind of talent, one must make allowances.

BEEBE HALL'S RAZZLE-DAZZLE LEMONADE FOR THE LAWNBOY

4 ounces of reconstituted lemon juice
7 teaspoons powdered sugar
16 ounce bottle of sparkling water
2 trays of ice cubes made with sparkling water

Combine lemon juice and powdered sugar in a pitcher. Stir. Fill the pitcher with ice cubes and pour in sparkling water. Watch it fizz!

Beebe was intrigued by recipes that could flame, fizzle, razzle and dazzle her. After The Lawnboy had finished mowing, she would bring out the lemonade for him, and pour the sparkling water into the glass so he could watch the 'snap, crackle, and pop.' It made him feel awkward each time she insisted he watch her 'lemonade/fireworks' show. After all, he was just thirsty.

---

[2] *Beebe's mother was suspected of arson many times, but once, when she was getting up in years and should have known better, she was caught red-handed and immediately booked on arson charges. She informed the judge that in her previous life, she was in on 'the storming of the Bastille', and all she could figure out was that she must have subconsciously and unconsciously re-enacted what had happened to her on that fateful day. Poor Louis, she continued, he didn't have a chance. She brought her French lineage charts to court and told the judge she could trace it back further if he needed proof. To further plead her case, she brought her elaborate family flambé recipes she always serves on Bastille Day, showed them to the judge and invited him over for the next Bastille Day dinner party. She boldly told him, "You'll change your mind about me once you taste my Flambe' Cherries Jubilee." The judge wasn't impressed and didn't buy it. However, things didn't turn out badly. Somehow Bunny Baxley's husband, Johnny, the brilliant smooth-talking lawyer, got Beebe's mother off with a slap on the wrist quicker than you could say Boom!*

MRS. ELMER STEELE

MRS. ELMER STEELE

Mrs. Elmer Steele, the honorable grand patron of numerous worthy, prestigious civic and cultural organizations, is truly an example of womanhood wonderment. Her unwavering commitment to worthy causes, her knack for organizing people, (even Bunny Baxley) and her fearless ability to steer any organization and any committee leaves her in a league of her own.

Some who are envious of her abilities have labeled her as being short-tempered, nosy, strong-willed, bossy, and one who is always ready to run with the ball even when it's not in her court. However, everyone agrees she is a paragon of morality who never deviates from the social code, and always gets done what she has promised to do, even though she is not the most yielding of ladies.

Her analytical mind is far superior to those of most males, including her husband, Mr. Elmer Steele, a well-respected philanthropist and well-known philanderer who goes to his office most days. Nobody really knows what his company is all about; he has never thought it necessary to tell anyone what it is he does, but everyone suspects it has to do with inherited railroad money and investments. Mr. Elmer Steele spends most of his time golfing, yachting and hunting fox – both ladies and animals.

With Mrs. Elmer Steele's generous and tireless contributions of time and energy, and Mr. and Mrs. Elmer Steele's generous monetary contribution to the causes Mrs. Elmer Steele deems worthy, she sets the standards for those who strive to make their communities a better place to live. She is a born leader.

MRS. ELMER STEELE'S LEMONADE RECIPE AND HER 10 COMMANDMENTS FOR THE LAWNBOY

1 cup lemon juice, freshly squeezed
2 quarts water
¾ cup white sugar

Combine the water and sugar. Heat on the stove until the sugar melts. Remove from heat, and add the lemon juice. Mix well and refrigerate. Garnish with an orange slice.

1) Remember to move the gutters; the grass is getting out of control underneath them. Perhaps you forgot to trim under them the last time. Also, trim around all of the trees and bushes, and of course, don't forget the mailbox.

2) The grass clippings all have to be bagged. The lawn bags are in the garage, and the ties should be in the box. Set the full bags in the regular place. Make sure you fill the bags. I don't want any frivolous waste.

3) Make doubly sure you pick up all the rocks on the boulevard before you mow that area. I do not want rocks shooting all over, or the blade to get dull.

4) There is a sprinkler in the front yard that appears to be broken. It's sticking up, and I do not want you to run over it under any condition. I have red flagged it. It's being fixed tomorrow.

5) Oh, and alternate the lines; of course you know that.

6) I will be leaving for my cookbook committee meeting. Oh my, and not to forget, I have some fresh lemonade in the kitchen for you. Make sure you wipe off your feet before you go into the kitchen. When you leave, shut and lock the door, and make sure you shut and lock the garage door.

7) Sweep the walkways and the driveway after you finish.

8) There will be $7.00 in an envelope for you. I will put it under the door mat on the side garage door. Make sure you take it. You earned it.

9) I will leave a second copy of these directions. Re-read them after you're done with your job to make sure you don't forget to do any of it.

10) Do you have any questions?

MRS. CHARLES CHATTERTON

MRS. CHARLES CHATTERTON

Anyone who has ever had the pleasure of meeting Mrs. Charles Chatterton, a tall, thin, fun-seeking resplendent lady, agrees she truly is someone who is in a league of her own, and not easily forgotten.

Charlotte's father came from a long line of very successful and sought-after furriers. Her family traveled the globe from Paris to Peking, from Moscow to Madrid, from Iceland to the Antarctica, to seek out and find the most exotic furs on the planet. As a young child, Charlotte loved traveling to far-flung places and immensely enjoyed socializing with other prominent people who 'minked and mingled.'

As teenagers, she and her childhood friend, Charlotte (nee Wadsworth) Bigsbee, watched the 1934 Chicago World's Fair synchronized swimming exhibition, and became consumed with the idea of joining and performing with a water ballet troupe of synchronized swimmers called the Marvelous Mermaids. Naturally, because of family prominence, this idea became nothing more than a childhood dream for both Charlotte and her friend, Charlotte Bigsbee. But her passion for traveling, wanting to be noticed and looking fit, was formed at an early age.

Charlotte found her perfect match in Charles Chatterton, a man who shared her goal to experience life at its largest, highest, newest and most exciting. By the time she married Charles Chatterton, he was already well-established in the gaming business, and was well-known from the Riviera to Las Vegas. With their hectic and far-flung lifestyle, Charles and Charlotte agreed that neither children nor poodles would fit in, or be necessary or needed.

Charlotte and Charles found it necessary and practical to own several homes away from home; but she has always loved her home on the lake the most. It is a place she rests,[3] relaxes, reconnects, swims and study fashion books and magazines while snuggled in her minks.

Charlotte is always fashionably dressed to the 'nines'. Whether she's in her Dior suits, or wrapped in one of her many sables with Paris labels, her appearance has always accentuated her significance. This lovely looking lady, who wisely keeps her cosmetics at hand, believes the adage that vanity is not a sin. Her coiffure is always dictated by the latest and most fashionable style down to the color and *guiches* on her cheeks. [4]

This splendid lady, who is an ardent follower of the Hollywood Diet,[5] is always willing to work with the other ladies on The Executives' Wives' Cookbook Committee when she is in town and physically able to help. She recently agreed to be First Vice President of the La La La La Lipstick Ball that her friends, Mrs. Stanley Bigsbee and Bunny Baxley, are co-chairing. She is truly a social success.

---

[3] *Mrs. Charles Chatterton was diagnosed with Narcolepsy in her early 20s. Only her closest friends know about her condition. Many who aren't privy to this information, but have seen her sometimes bizarre behavior, shrug it off thinking she's had 'one too many.'*
[4] *Her friends tell her she looks like Carol Burnett.*
[5] *The Hollywood Diet is sometimes called the Grapefruit Diet. The diet consists of eating ½ grapefruit for 18 days. She is also known to crush her diet pills in her Jell-0.*

MRS. CHARLES CHATTERTON'S PERFECT LEMONADE
FOR THE LAWNBOY AND HERSELF

6-7 lemons, depending upon the size of the lemons
1 cup white sugar
7 cups of ice cold tap water

Cut the lemons in half, and juice them in a juicer. In a large pitcher, combine the lemon juice, sugar and water. Refrigerate for several hours. Thoroughly stir the lemonade before serving.

Mrs. Charles Chatterton's lake home is grand and comfortable, protected by judicious planting. Her lawn, which overlooks the lake, is large, lush and lovely.

It takes The Lawnboy at least two hours to mow her lawn. She always makes a pitcher of lemonade for both her and The Lawnboy on sizzling days that can be so punishing. She invariably tells him, "You're such a trooper."

With her Vanity Fair *magazine in hand, she entertains herself by reclining in her lawn chair on her patio to read. Periodically she peers over the top of her 'readers' to watch him work. Sometimes when The Lawnboy has to ask her a question, she appears to be sleeping, but she quickly wakes up and says something like, "I wish you were 30 years younger."*

After he finishes, she stops reading and drinks a glass of lemonade with him. She enjoys watching the metamorphosis. Everything is looking beautiful. Such a sight!

12

MRS. STANLEY BIGSBEE

MRS. STANLEY BIGSBEE

Mrs. Stanley Bigsbee was the daughter of a very famous chemist/doctor whose life-enhancing patented formulas had a marked influence on her and others. As a young child, she watched as her father tirelessly worked to create formulas that would help his wife, a lady who had trouble coping with all the demands of life.

Because of her mother's unfortunate conditions, Mrs. Stanley Bigsbee, or Charlotte as her closest friends called her, spent much of her free time with her father, traveling with him and her nanny as he presented papers at prestigious universities around the world. She was mesmerized as she watched her father perform experiments by mixing chemicals in test tubes. At an early age, Charlotte showed her brilliant curiosity by asking her father to use some test tubes to teach her how to mix chemicals to create lipstick. Her father realized that lipstick, not chemistry, was her passion but he was smitten with her curiosity.

As she became older, she was interested in other things, especially Stanley Bigsbee. Young, ambitious Stanley, a noted chemist in his own right, bought a large pharmaceutical company with his mentor, Charlotte's father. It was a perfect match for everyone concerned - intellectually, emotionally and especially financially. As Charlotte said to Stanley before they married, "I want to make it perfectly clear that I need to maintain a distinctive style of life." Stanley understood, and honored her request.

With all that in mind it is no wonder she was nominated by her peers to co-chair, with Bunny Baxley, The Executives' Wives' Cookbook Committee's La La La La Lipstick Ball.

The Lipstick Ball, so cleverly and brilliantly coined, 'The La La La La Lipstick Ball' by Mrs. Stanley Bigsbee, was held to honor the ladies who had worked so tirelessly on The Executives' Wives' Cookbook Committee and, of course, to raise funds for worthy causes.

Mrs. Stanley Bigsbee was the perfect co-chair. Major events, like the La La La La Lipstick Ball took a toll on many ladies, especially while socializing. Invariably, it left them feeling anxious and unsteady. Mrs. Stanley Bigsbee, who was no stranger to those feelings, and who was always thinking of others, made sure she had fabulous pharmaceuticals that (thanks to her father) were readily available.

With all the overwhelming trials that Mrs. Stanley Bigsbee endured in her formative years, she still greets her friends with her signature salutation, "You delicious darling, do I have lipstick on my teeth?" No matter what the trouble or circumstance, she remained upbeat, loyal and could always be counted on to lend an ear, pill or martini to any and every one of her friends who had emotional or physical pain.

MRS. STANLEY BIGSBEE'S HARD-CORE LEMONADE FOR THE LAWNBOY

2 ounces of vodka
juice of 1 lemon
2 teaspoons sugar
½ cup soda water
½ cup regular water

Mix all the ingredients and pour into a tall glass. Leave room for lots of ice.

The Lawnboy knew when he came to work on Mrs. Stanley Bigsbee's grounds, he would be subject to her nonsensical ramblings. With drink in hand, she would, more often than not, come out of her house, greet him, wink at him, and with a slurred voice say, "Hi, you dearie little thing, you're cute as a button. Oh, aren't I naughty? You know what to do."

Stanley says you have to rake the beach. I need to go freshen up my pedicure. My daughter, Elizabeth,[6] made some really delicious lemonade just for you. I think she has her eye on you.

---

[6] *Elizabeth made sure when she served The Lawnboy, it was nonalcoholic lemonade.*

MRS. MOLLY McCURDLE

MRS. MOLLY McCURDLE

Mrs. Molly McCurdle can be best described as a pretty, prissy, fragile and flighty lady who has a sweet, sweet, disposition. Born with an abundance of energy, she is a burst of brilliant sunshine, and a bouquet of beauty. It can be truthfully said that this lovely lady was born without any hard edges, or 'mean bones' in her body. Her passions for growing exotic orchids, and giving workshops on the 'art of opening and immersing oneself in the powerful aroma of gardenia buds', are the talk of the social circles.

Molly's father was a very important diplomat who held many prestigious government jobs. That being said, it was a given that the family moved often to various foreign countries. Because Molly's father traveled extensively, and was away from home for long extended periods of time, Molly, an only child, was raised by her mother.

Molly's mother, a Southern Belle, in the true sense of the word, often-times longed to be back at her childhood plantation home to bask in the Southern genteel living that was in her blood, even though she knew it was impossible due to her husband's important government position. She did the very best she could, and took her child-rearing responsibilities seriously, schooling Molly in things such as beauty and ballet, curtsies and cuteness, charm and cheerleading, flounces and flowers, grace and gowns, pink and pretty, and all other most important and imperative Southern rituals and social graces.

One must add that Molly's mother was mentally fragile. Her psychiatrist said it was from the trauma of being separated from her Southern lifestyle. She coped by living in a fantasy world, and projected this surreal sense of reality to Molly. Unfortunately, Molly, at a very early age, became empress of her own make-believe world, and was diagnosed with the Peter Pan syndrome. Molly's psychiatrist later told her that her

Peter Pan syndrome was exasperated by her bout with Scarlet Fever. This, in turn, started a vicious cycle and Molly became a hypochondriac among other things.

This condition didn't seem to matter to Molly's husband, Kent McCurdle. Kent, also born and reared in a prominent Southern family where money and roots ran deep, met Molly when she was presented at her debutante at a 'still-talked about' cotillion ball. [7]She was very young when Kent met her, but, at first glance he instinctively knew that someday she would become his wife, and she did. You can only imagine how thrilled both Molly's mother and Kent's mother were when they discovered they had the same sterling silver flatware pattern. [8]As Molly's mother said to Molly upon learning about Mrs. McCurdle's sterling flatware, "Even if you don't have the utmost of warm fuzzy feelings for Kent, trust me, it's a match made in heaven."

After the betrothal of Kent and Molly was properly announced and celebrated, it took two years and three months before the wedding plans were perfectly choreographed. With the hope chest filled with porcelain china and 'hope', and Molly's trousseau was completed with fancy French *pegnoirs* and bed jackets, Kent, who was taking over his father's cotton empire, knew Molly, her mother, and his mother would not include him in the plans, including the honeymoon.[9] As Molly told Kent, "I've traveled and lived all over the world. For our honeymoon I just want to go to Disneyland for a week, to fill-up on fun, fairies and fu-fu." Kent who called his beloved betrothed, 'My Lady-Muffy' agreed.

After the honeymoon, Molly quickly realized that due to business, Kent, like her father, would be absent a great deal of the time. After a most difficult pregnancy and birth, Molly and Kent became the adoring parents of twin daughters – Rose Margaret

---

[7] *Molly's mother was relieved that Molly was nominated and chosen to be a debutante at the cotillion ball that, according to her mother, 'was the only one.' Because the family was living abroad for periods of time, and Molly's mother wasn't around to be on the right committees, she hoped her family connections were enough for Molly's nomination. They were, and everyone was relieved.*

[8] *Reed and Barton, Francis I pattern which has twenty-eight pieces of fruit on the knife handle alone!*

[9] *Kent McCurdle didn't have any choice. The only important thing for him was that his bride-to-be was born south of the Mason-Dixon Line, and she was.*

and Violet Margaret. Molly, with her mother, mother-in-law, and entourage of nannies and helpers, all helped with raising the twins, and the ladies knew they were doing a brilliant job when they were able to boast that the twins, who were always dressed like matching dolls, had mastered the St. John's Bow[10] even before they were out of their walkers.

Like her mother, as Molly got older, her make-believe world became more real. She convinced Kent they needed a new home, built in the architectural style of a grand Southern plantation, complete with a conservatory for her orchids, sweeping grand staircase, large and grand ballroom, and a fairy tale play room for the girls. Kent agreed, but what he didn't know, but could only suspect, and later learned, was that Molly had the fairy tale room actually built for herself.

Her twins, Rose and Violet, played in the room during the day. At night, when Kent was home in bed and snoring loudly, Molly would sneak out of their bedroom and into the enchanted fairy tale room where she would indulge in her own fantasy world surrounded by tiaras, pom-poms, ballet bars, fairy costumes, glitter, child-size tea sets, magic wands, jars of fairy dust, music boxes, snow globes, and jewelry boxes with porcelain ballerinas that popped up and turned and danced every time she opened them. In her room and in her mind, she could go 'bare

naked in her thoughts' and fly around like Mary Poppins, or pretend she was gowned and glorious like dark-haired green-eyed Scarlet O'Hara was, when she descended the grand staircase at Tara.

---

[10] *For those who are unfamiliar with the St. John's Bow, picture an anorexic-looking dying swan, which hasn't had food or water for days upon days.*

Once, when Kent, was at home and had awakened himself with his own loud snoring, he realized Molly was not in bed and he was covered in dust. [11] After wandering around their large 'plantation', he finally found her sound asleep on the white provincial canopy bed, dressed in a child-like pink lace ruffled fairy *pegnoir* and a matching pink tulle tu tu, in the fantasy room. Tented over her chest was the book, Gone with the Wind,[12] opened to the page where Rhett said to Scarlett, "Frankly, my dear, I don't give a damn."

After that episode, he became a little worried about her obsessions with 'la la land' and her state of mind. He gently convinced her that she should get involved in community affairs. He convinced her that she would be a natural on The Executives' Wives' Cookbook Committee, and through his connections, he personally saw to it that she would become a member.[13]

Molly enthusiastically embraced The Executives' Wives' Cookbook Committee, especially when she found out that the committee had chosen Puppies and Children in Distress, as their charitable cause. She worked tirelessly to ensure the project would be the smashing success that it turned out to be.

Thankfully, her mother and mother-in-law took her twin daughters under their tutelage and made sure that when Molly was engrossed in the cookbook project, they would see to it that the twins were chauffeured to charm school, ballet class, cheerleading practice, piano lessons, social manners school, debutante school, and all other important schools and things in life.

MRS. MOLLY MCCURDLE'S PRETTY PINK LEMONADE FOR THE LAWNBOY

3 ½ cups of watermelon, chunked
½ cup spring water
¼ cup sugar
¼ cup lime juice
4 tablespoons of lemon juice

Cut watermelon into small chunks and place in a blender. Add the other ingredients and blend everything on high speed. Chill. When serving, pour into tall glasses and garnish each drink with a lemon leaf and an edible flower such as a pansy.

Mrs. Molly McCurdle was a gracious lady. She would always thank him for the effort he put in to making her lawn beautiful. Her lemonade, which was always served in her gazebo, was like her – pretty, pink and infused with delicious flavors and garnished with flowers. She made The Lawnboy feel appreciated. She once told him, "I would love to have a son just like you."

---

[11] *Whenever she could, Molly would sprinkle fairy dust on Kent when he was sound asleep. It brought her comfort to know that the fairies were protecting him.*

[12] *Molly was thirty years old before she was confronted with the truth that Tara was a fictitious place. She cried when she came to the realization, and was upset that her mother had never told her the truth about Tara, or how painful menstrual cramps can really get, and the hindrances they involve.*

[13] *Kent's connection was Bunny Baxley's husband, Johnny, the brilliant lawyer and friend who sees that what needs to be done for his friends, gets done.*

MRS. GRANT GOLDMAN-HUES

MRS. GRANT GOLDMAN-HUES

When it comes down to personal appearances, Mrs. Grant Goldman-Hues lives and breathes the adage that presentation is everything. From her meticulously coiffed hair, to her elegant Chanel-couture clothes, to her lavender colored lips and eyes, to her dazzling diamonds and exquisite jewelry, she is, indeed, a rare gem.

One could say that Mrs. Goldman-Hues, or Harriett Helen, as her birth certificate reads, was born into a privileged life that shaped her destiny. Her father, a Russian immigrant, became a most famous and sought-after diamond and gem dealer. She and her mother would often go on buying trips to Antwerp, Belgium, and London, England, with her father, where she was exposed to cut, clarity, color, carat, conspicuousness and competitiveness.

Conveniently, she fell in love and married Grant Hues, the son of her father's business partner. Even though Harriett 'hoped for the Hope' she was satisfied with the rare, flawless ring he presented her, one of the many countless, beautiful pieces of jewelry he continuously bestowed upon her.

Indeed, Mrs. Grant Goldman-Hues looks lovely to behold, but looks can be deceiving. This fiercely competitive lady secretly tries to 'one-up' her friends not only in her jewelry, and loveliness, but also in her recipes and chess skills.[14]

She wasn't prone to bragging, and really had no need to, considering her envious circumstances and lifestyle. However, she did 'name drop' once when she was entertaining The Executives' Wives' Cookbook Committee. As everyone has always known, she was an avid chess player. When she got to see Boris Spassky compete and win the 1955 junior chess championship in Antwerp, Belgium, she let down her guard and announced that she not only watched him win, but that he was a not-so-distant relative of her husband, Grant.

As she matured, she became slightly paranoid, a condition that naturally manifested itself in diamond dealers and their wives. She once suspected that her housekeeper tried on her 14 carat diamond necklace, and she fired her immediately.

This regal lady is truly a rare kaleidoscope of color, brilliance, shape and form.

[14] As a child, Mrs. Grant Goldman-Hues learned to play chess from her father. He always told her she dazzled him with her brilliance and beauty. Once when he came home from a buying trip, young Harriett thought it would be fun to substitute the ivory chess pieces using her mother's finest jewels. She cleverly used her mother's largest diamonds for the king and queen, her pigeon-blood rubies for the bishops, her cornflower-blue sapphires for the knights, her square cut green emeralds for the rooks, and the large, beautiful amethysts (her favorite color) for the pawns. Her dad was so impressed with her creativity, he bought her a 20 carat diamond tiara that she put to good use when she was nominated homecoming queen of her high school.

MRS. GRANT GOLDMAN-HUES'
VINTAGE LEMONADE
FOR THE LAWNBOY

6-7 lemons
1 ½ cups white sugar
1 ½ quarts of spring water

With a small knife, peel the lemons. Section them
into slices. Put the lemon rinds in a bowl, and
sprinkle the sugar over them. Let this mixture set for
1 to 2 hours. Bring the spring water to a boil, and
then pour the boiled water over the lemon rind/sugar
mixture. Cool. Squeeze the lemons into the lemon
rind/sugar mixture. Stir well, and pour contents into a
beautiful cut glass pitcher. Chill well.

*Mrs. Grant Goldman-Hues loves to host elaborate
brunches for her dearest, intimate circle of friends. Her
friends, even though dear, are envious of her chess-playing
ability, her lovely lawn, and of course, her jewels.*

*Thanks to her gardeners and The Lawnboy, her lawn is as
green as her rare emerald gems, and as immaculately
manicured as her fingers and toes. When the Lawnboy
mowed her lawn on the day she hosted her brunch for The
Executives' Wives' Cookbook Committee, he knew it had to
be more than perfect. After he had finished mowing, she
scoured every inch of her lawn as if she were looking for a
lost diamond. When she has deemed it 'perfect', she said to
him, "Now I will get you a glass of lemonade." She always
serves him lemonade in a beautiful, monogrammed, sterling
silver cup.*

MRS. SAMUEL SQUIRE

24

MRS. SAMUEL SQUIRE

Mrs. Samuel Squire, a genteel and intelligent lady who was born with a 'silver spoon' in her mouth, possesses an innate sense of upper crust sophistication and quiet dignity. Everyone who is privileged to be invited to her lovely manor, is in awe of her beautiful, rare, properly marked English silver collection and other valuable antiques that she inherited from her famous English ancestors. Her ability to host a proper English high tea, in the most gracious and refined manner, rivals those thrown by Mrs. E.O Bittleduke, and Mrs. Michael Stellar.

Mrs. Squire's husband, Samuel, who was named after both Samuel Adams, a signer of the Declaration of Independence, and William Samuel Johnson, a signer of the Constitution, is her biggest supporter and admirer. Appropriately, they met the year she was chosen to be the 4th of July Regatta Queen, and he was chosen to be the commodore of the Republican Revolutionary Regatta Flotilla. She was smitten by him because they had so much in common. He could trace his lineage back to the first Lord of the Manor of Hanbury on his paternal side and to Duke William of Normandy [15] on his maternal side. He was in possession of his very own personal 'Squire' Coat of Arms, which she knew was legal tender and could and did make her feel secure and validated.

The Squires are generous supporters of numerous prestigious and exclusive organizations that preserve and promote historical homes, blue-blood lineages, Scottish lodges and the Grand Old Party. They travel several times a year to Great Britain for holidays and to see their daughter who married a titled Duke. They fly both the United States' and Union Jack flags at their summer home.

She celebrates and acknowledges their family's illustrious ancestral lineage, and her love for the United States, Great Britain and the Republican Party by hosting numerous spirited patriotic parties from May until September. These parties are indeed daunting and exhausting, but her commitment and contribution to benefit mankind is unwavering. For all she does, we salute her!

THE *SQUIRE'S* PATRIOTIC LEMONADE FOR THE LAWNBOY AND THEIR REPUBLICAN GUESTS

10 cups of water
3 ¼ cups of sugar
6 lemons
1 ¾ cups of Maine blueberries
red food coloring

In a saucepan, boil the water and sugar, then chill the syrup concoction in the refrigerator. Juice six lemons and add to chilled syrup mixture. Puree the Maine blueberries and add to the lemonade. Pour in punch bowl.

Pour 1 teaspoon red food coloring in a quart of water. Freeze in ice cubes trays. Float the festive-colored red ice cubes in the punch bowl.

The day before the Squire's yearly 4th of July patriotic party, The Lawnboy knew he would be asked to help the gardener get the expansive grounds in tip top shape, and on the day of the party he would be asked to help serve with the caterer.

The gardener's duty was to fluff and quaff the flower gardens. He had to pay special attention to the garden that was in the shape of the American Flag with red, white and blue plantings.

The Lawnboy was instructed to make sure the alternate lines were cut in exact precision. Mr. Samuel Squire

---

[14] *Samuel's maternal ancestors were the owners of a grand and gracious manorial estate in Devonshire, England. Mr. and Mrs. Samuel Squire's manor was fashioned after their ancestral home in Devonshire, even though, through research, he found out some of his early ancestors owed back-taxes, and had shamelessly sold their herd of Devonshire Bovines to pay their overdue taxes.*

watched with intense scrutiny, both the gardener and The Lawnboy, to make sure their task was perfectly executed to his exact specifications.

The flag staff was busy cleaning the flag poles and oiling the chains, and making sure the flags —American, Revolutionary and The National Society of the Washington Family Descendants' flags- were ready to fly.

Mrs. Samuel Squire, in her usual curt manner, instructed the caterer and his staff on proper attire, other important protocol rules such as being attentive to guests' needs, and most importantly, 'do not speak to unless spoken to.' She emphasized that it was of utmost importance to follow her rules because their guests would include card-carrying Republicans, true patriots and blue-bloods who had the right pedigree charts.

With a glass of lemonade in hand, she walked to the North bar where The Lawnboy was setting up. She handed him the glass, slipped a ten dollar bill in his shirt pocket and said "Enjoy." He felt appreciated.

MRS. MICHAEL STELLAR

MRS. MICHAEL STELLAR

Mrs. Michael Stellar, or Sarah Elizabeth Rose, [16] the name which was lovingly bestowed upon this only child of a very prominent and well-known, well-connected Southern family, is as pretty and petite as a delicate and dainty hand-painted rose bud, bone china tea cup; but don't let perceptions surprise you.

This lovely lady is known to get up at sunrise, regardless of the elements outside, and don her signature garden clothes-white starched blouse, and linen Capri pants. With clippers in hand and a driving purpose in mind, she firmly, but gingerly, cuts every hybrid tea rose that is perfectly-shaped and perfectly-ready; and all this before her gardener arrives. Such ambition and determination! [17]

Mrs. Michael Stellar is no stranger to beautifully decorated homes with sweeping verandas framed by multiple rose gardens, and white picket fences engulfed in fragrant sweet peas, gardenias, azaleas, and showy lilies. Her father's love of show horses and all things connected to equestrian life-style and Southern comforts and 'Southern Comfort' made an impact. It introduced her to a side of life that wasn't part of her mother's world, but a world that made her stronger and more forgiving. How fortunate for her!

Sipping Mint Juleps, sweetened teas, pink-colored lemonade, Pink Squirrels, Pink Cosmopolitans, Pink Blushes, while enjoying high teas, and gracious living was part of her mother's world; so were fine foods, and everything beautiful and French. So, it is no surprise that Mrs. Michael Stellar, with her sweet and endearing disposition, greets her guests in a self-posed manner, and makes them feel comfortable and important in her lovely home which is overflowing with French Provincial antiques, French art and ornate sconces fashioned of wrought metal. Sheer loveliness!

More importantly, she belongs to the right social circles and religious affiliations, and shows her dedication by taking her pivotal role in her family activities very seriously. She blushes when her husband, Michael, an accomplished architect whose genius is sought after world-wide, tells everyone how fortunate he is to have had his American Beauty Rose, as he endearingly calls her, introduced to him at her debutante. Her friends say her only defect is that she doesn't have one. It doesn't get more inspiring than that!

Mrs. Michael Stellar was tickled pink when The Executive's Wives' Cookbook Committee nominated her to co-chair the Butterfly Ball with Mrs. E.O. Bittleduke. It wasn't an accident that she was asked. They all know her abilities when it comes to marvelous floral arrangements and proper seating charts. She knows

---

[16] *She was appropriately christened Sarah Elizabeth because as her father said, "We not only have a princess, but a queen." Rose was the Confirmation name she chose for herself. It was all lovely!*
[17] *It doesn't end here. Even when she is bone tired from an exhausting day, she makes sure she writes in both her diary and her garden journal. Such persistence!*

how to make sure everything is as pretty and proper, and flitty and flighty as an ethereal butterfly drinking nectar out of pink tea roses in a well-tended rose garden on beautiful summer days. They know Mrs. Michael Stellar would and could rise to the challenge of chairing the glorious ball, without so much as having to have a pillbox in her purse when things became hectic. They were confident that all she needed was her rosy-pink outlook, a Jackie Kennedy pink pillbox hat and, as is said, the rest is history.

MRS. MICHAEL STELLAR'S
ELEGANT STRAWBERRY LEMONADE
FOR THE LAWNBOY

8 cups of water
1 ½ cups white sugar
¾ cup lemon juice, freshly squeezed
2 cups of medium-sized firm, red strawberries

Combine water and sugar. Boil for approximately 2 minutes, being careful not to scorch the mixture. Chill the mixture in the refrigerator for at least two hours. Cut lemons, remove the seeds with kitchen tweezers, and juice the lemons. Pour the chilled sugar water and the lemon juice into a tall, glass pitcher and stir. Right before serving, add some of the strawberries that have been washed, de-stemmed, hulled and air-dried, to the lemonade in the pitcher. Put three 'well-appointed' strawberries in each glass.

The Lawnboy knew when he mowed the gracious Mrs. Michael Stellar's lawn he would have company. The lovely Mrs. Michael Stellar always came out of her house, small pruning shears in her pink-gloved hands, to tend to her beloved tea roses. Dressed in her linen Capri pants, crisp white blouse, garden garnets, and her ribbon and flower-bedecked straw hat, she mastered grace, beauty, elegance and charm as she diligently pruned and cut away in her rose garden. After The Lawnboy would finish mowing, she would bring him a glass of her signature, pink lemonade which was topped off with sweet, juicy, luscious strawberries. While he drank his lemonade, she would cut a

rose, gently caress its petals, indulging in its fragrance, and with a soft pleasing voice gaze at him and say, "This rose is the American Beauty." He looked at Mrs. Michael Stellar, who was dressed from top to toe in her 'flower frillys', and wondered if this whole scenario was inappropriate.

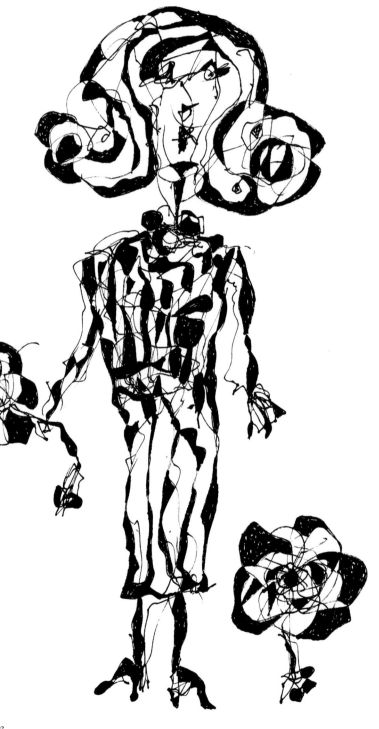

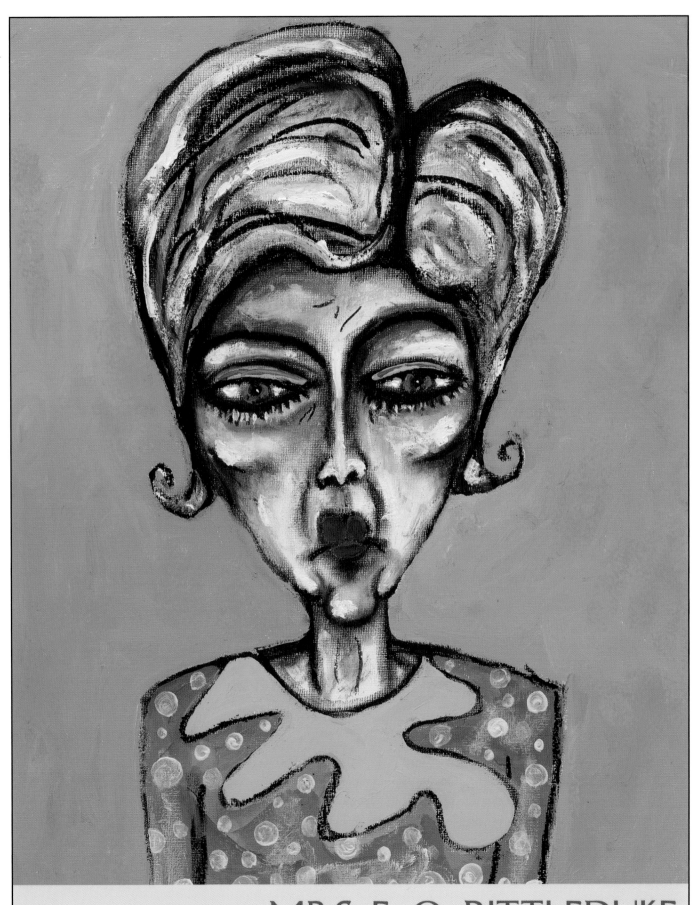

MRS. E. O. BITTLEDUKE

MRS. E.O. BITTLEDUKE

Mrs. E.O. Bittleduke, wife of Dr. E.O. Bittleduke, a successful and noted gynecologist, is a doctor in her own right; i.e. she has always had the uncanny ability to surprisingly diagnose her family's and friends' ailments before a doctor or specialist could confirm it. It is no surprise this bright, elegant lady has this remarkable, almost clairvoyant talent. After all, both her parents and her grandfathers were famous physicians who dined with the 'M' [18] brothers.

She was a gifted and inquisitive child; a voracious reader of medical books, encyclopedias and science journals. She decided early on that she would not pursue a career in medicine because of the demanding hours of the profession and the toll it takes on a family. After graduating from Vassar, this Phi Beta Kappa member decided to mold her life to fit the pattern of her husband's career. It proved to be a wise choice.

Throughout their illustrious careers, the Bittledukes have always generously contributed time, enthusiasm and money to numerous worthy charitable causes. Shortly after Dr. E.O. Bittleduke retired, he was diagnosed with early stages of forgetfulness. [19] Mrs. E.O. Bittleduke, the undaunted, elegant and bright lady she is known to be, rose to the occasion and learned to singularly handle every task needed to make sure their lives were as normal as they could be, considering their devastating and unfortunate circumstances.

As you can imagine, she is thrust into his life's affairs in more ways than one. Once a week, she engages a nurse to watch her husband so she can go to his office to make sure the medical charts and the information of his long-time, private patients are safe. Even though he has given up his practice, she wants to make sure there are no stones unturned. Painstakingly gleaning through his patients' records, she has found some surprising information about some of her dearest friends. However, this lady of integrity honors the Hippocratic Oath and keeps everyone's secrets to herself. After all, she justifies to herself, what she is doing is invaluable, because it is a tool she can use to better help diagnose her friends' problems.

Even though Mrs. E.O. Bittleduke is consumed with her husband's illness and affairs, they still manage to lead a somewhat normal life. She and 'The Doctor', with the help of his private-care nurse and The Lawnboy, take trips to England twice a year so she can continue her passion of looking for and buying valuable, English silver pieces.

MRS. E.O. BITTLEDUKE'S HEALTHY LEMONADE FOR THE LAWNBOY AND 'THE DOCTOR'

2 cups distilled water
¾ cup brown sugar
¾ cup white sugar
1 ½ teaspoons honey

8 additional cups of distilled water
2 cups lemon juice, freshly squeezed
maraschino cherries

In a saucepan, combine 2 cups of distilled water, brown sugar, white sugar and honey. Bring this mixture to a boil, and simmer for 10 minutes, stirring occasionally and watching carefully so the mixture doesn't scorch. Cool the combined ingredients and chill.

Mix together 8 cups of distilled water, and 2 cups of juice from squeezed, unblemished lemons. Pour this

---

[18] *The 'M' stands for the Mayo Brothers. Mrs. E.O. Bittleduke is uncomfortable with name dropping and is known as a quiet braggart. However, we thought it necessary you understand that her family is more than just famous; they are prestigious, too.*
[19] *This diagnosis came the year before Mrs. E.O. Bittleduke was asked to co-chair The Butterfly Ball with Mrs. Michael Stellar. When Dr. E.O. Bittleduke told his wife he was looking forward to The Moth Ball, she knew it was time for him to retire.*

mixture into a glass pitcher, stir, and then add the chilled, cooked syrup. Chill in the refrigerator for several hours before serving. Garnish each drink with a Maraschino cherry.

This is the lemonade recipe Mrs. E.O. Bittleduke used when serving both The Lawnboy and her retired husband, Dr. E.O. Bittleduke. She deemed it a 'healthier' recipe than most lemonade recipes. She liked to stir it up with a thermometer.

At this point in his life, Dr. E.O. Bittleduke didn't know and didn't care if his drinks were healthy or not. As long as his drinks were garnished with Maraschino cherries, he was content.
Mrs. E.O. Bittleduke, the poor soul, was doing everything in her power to see if anything could help him with his forgetfulness.

Before The Lawnboy started mowing, he would greet Dr. E.O. Bittleduke who was always outside sitting in his favorite Adirondack chair. The Lawnboy would patiently listen to 'The Doctor's' stories, which were the same every week, including the stories about the Catskill Mountains, where he and Barbara had honeymooned. The Lawnboy was amused by Dr. E.O. Bittleduke and his sometimes inappropriate chatter.

Mrs. E.O. Bittleduke would make The Lawnboy nervous. When he was mowing, she would watch him through the curtained windows. He just knew she was not only watching to make sure 'The Doctor' didn't wander on to the neighbor's lawn, but also needed to make sure the lines were mowed straight.

At the 'appropriate' time, and in a very unassuming manner, Mrs. E.O. Bittleduke would bring the lemonades to the patio on a silver tray. She would pour the lemonades and graciously say, "Let's all sit down and relax now. I don't want any of us to overheat."

KATRINA CANFIELD

This ambitious, chic, classy lady knows where she wants to go in life, and goes. Whether she's jet setting to Europe to shop or buy art, or off to New York for the latest Guggenheim exhibit, or down to Acapulco to watch the cliff divers, this tall, slender, savvy lady is a seasoned globe trotter. Bursting with energy, she is highly motivated and meets her self-imposed demands with spirit and success.

Both Katrina and her husband, Blake, were born into a chic, socially connected, cosmopolitan life. Blake, a successful architect and Katrina, a polished art connoisseur, are considered 'cafe society', modish and way ahead of their times.

They enjoy entertaining and never tire of showing off their Mies van der Rohe designed, glass home, their marble pool, expansive grounds and lawns, their enormous, modern art collection, and their hand-blown, glass birds from Scandinavia.

Whether she's donned in Dior, or dressed in 'pool-party chic', Katrina is a minimalist, who knows styles and wears them with attitude. She and her husband, Blake, are sought out as guests at numerous social functions, both with friends, and through Blake's business connections.

Katrina and Blake have always belonged to many social circles, and the ladies on The Executives' Wives' Cookbook Committee do not consist of their favorite people. She joined The Executives' Wives' Cookbook Committee for three reasons; and for three reasons only. They were: (1) Mrs. Christina Pebbleworth-Stafford, her rival, was on the committee. (2) She strongly believed in organizations that supported animal rights and she knew The Executives' Wives' Cookbook Committee was on to this cause. (3) Her husband, Blake, constantly reassured her that the ladies on The Executives' Wives' Cookbook Committee had connections that were invaluable to his business, and she was reaping the benefits. So, she begrudgingly continued to be part of the circle.

After the party they threw for The Executives' Wives' Cookbook Committee, she told her husband, Blake, "If you want me to continue on this committee, perhaps you can buy me a David Hockney painting, or Roy Lichtenstein's painting, *Drowning Girl*. I would change it to: I don't care; I would rather sink than call The Executives' Wives' Cookbook Committee for help."

KATRINA CANFIELD'S HAWAIIAN POOL PARTY LEMONADE FOR THE LAWNBOY

1 can frozen lemonade (6 ounces)
1 can pineapple juice (12 ounces)
1 can apricot nectar (12 ounces)
12 ounces ginger ale
crushed ice
lime slices

Mix together and pour over crushed ice. Add lime slices for garnish.

Katrina Canfield loved to entertain outside, and was a 'pool-patio person.' When The Lawnboy came to mow, he knew mowing her yard was secondary to cleaning and hosing down her pool decks, washing the patio furniture, stocking the pool refrigerators, and cleaning the grills. After he finished his work, she always had huge glasses of lemonade ready for him and said "You've worked hard, so take off your shirt, jump in, and enjoy." He knew he was the only one who was privileged enough to be asked to swim in her pool.

MARTHA PAYNE

38

MARTHA PAYNE

Martha Payne can most aptly be described as a lady in rather striking circumstances. She studied art at Vassar, and the highest of honors were bestowed upon this amazing introspective lady while she endured ill health, and other unfortunate obstacles that people, not of her caliber, would certainly find insurmountable.

Her husband, Dr. Theodore Payne III, a well-known and well-respected psychiatrist who graduated *summa cum laude* from Yale, is a highly regarded master practitioner of the Jacques Marie-Émile Lacan school of psychiatry. His life-long dream was finally realized when he discovered why his wife, Martha, froze in horror, and exhibited confusing and bewildering behavior every time she heard the sound of ice cubes crackling.[20]

However, as Dr. Payne quickly found out, diagnosing Martha's problem was just the tip of the iceberg. Treating it was a whole other challenge. He relentlessly and tirelessly tried everything to make her life normal and comfortable. He encouraged her to take still-life art classes. That didn't help much. Other times, when he can tell she is crumbling, he whisks her away on extended holidays. Sometimes this works for a while, but usually not. He coaches and prompts her to stay involved in their prominent social circles, and constantly reassures her he has access to medicinal helpers whenever she is too overwhelmed and feels shipwrecked. This is an effective therapy, even though he sometimes just gives her a pink sugar pill.

Most of her friends characterize her as a lady of soft spoken dignity. They know she is more than willing to help with causes when she is up to the task at hand. As Mrs. Elmer Steele said to Mrs. Michael Stellar when Martha missed two very important committee meetings for the Puppies and Children in Distress Charity, "Poor dear, she has awfully good intentions. They just never pan out."

Even Martha realizes that she deserves better out of life. Once when she was coming out of one of her situations, she said to her husband, "Things like this aren't supposed to happen to people like me."

MARTHA PAYNE'S MOTHER'S 'PUCKER' LEMONADE FOR THE LAWNBOY

6 to 7 cups water
¾ cup of white sugar
½ teaspoon salt
¾ cup lemon juice
lemon rinds

In a saucepan, combine the water, sugar and salt. Bring to a boil, making sure the mixture doesn't scorch. Chill the mixture for several hours.

Juice 5-6 lemons and cut the rinds of two lemons into strips. Mix everything together, stir vigorously, and pour into a pitcher.

Martha Payne was a proper lady, who always seemed oddly disturbed, aloof, reserved and hard to read. Sometimes when The Lawnboy came to mow, he was greeted by her housekeeper who vaguely announced that Martha was away. At times, Martha was home when The Lawnboy came, and she would politely tell him to knock on the door when he was finished so she could give him a glass of lemonade. She never engaged him in idle chatter, but always paid him well. She always managed to smile when she appropriately complimented him on his work.

Martha's husband would make the lemonade, because Martha was too frightened to use the stove.
Because of Martha's malady, she did not dare to put ice cubes in the glasses of lemonade. In fact, it was even a struggle for her to open the refrigerator door and take the pitcher out for pouring the lemonade into the glasses.

---

[20] *After several years of study, Dr. Payne theorized that Martha couldn't tolerate the sound of ice cubes crackling because her mother, a Titanic survivor who never recovered mentally from the ordeal, passed on her angst to Martha while she was developing in the womb. He still hasn't figured out why she doesn't like fire or stoves, but it is a challenging problem he works on day and night.*

MRS. CHRISTINA PEBBLEWORTH-STAFFORD

MRS. CHRISTINA PEBBLEWORTH-STAFFORD

Mrs. Christina Pebbleworth-Stafford is by any standard a lady of great influence and quality who can be best described as a complete octave on a C major scale - classy, chic, composed, cosmopolitan, connected, cultured, 'chaneled and 'coutured'.[21] This exceptional lady, who is a fantastic mixture of wealth and wants, has the finesse and vision to make sure her wants, wishes and tastes are perfectly attuned to her high standards.

She truly is an embellishment to the family's glory,[22] and a steward of their limitless trust. She studied French and art history at Radcliff where she met and married David, a fabulously wealthy Harvard graduate. He is both a gentlemen and scholar. With their generous monetary contributions, his family helped to set the high and lofty standards that helped to make Harvard the iconic institution that it is today.

This polished, contemporary art connoisseur is at home surrounded by her paintings and objects d'art. Her exquisite residence is so large her guests often get lost. She entertains numerous wealthy and distinguished people, and even has a yearly dinner for both her American and European fashion consultants.

The Pebbleworth-Staffords travel to Paris and Milan at least four times a year to attend the fashion runway shows, to dine and to rejuvenate in refinement. With their aristocratic exclusiveness, they are always welcomed and personally greeted and acknowledged at Maxim's and all other fine Parisian restaurants and hotels. Such jet setters!

Mrs. Christina Pebbleworth-Stafford's manners are reserved and formal, and she sometimes comes across as cold, forbidding, haughty and nonconforming; that is unless she is under the 'Chanel spell'. An ardent fan, of Coco Chanel's couture lines, she readily and enthusiastically shares her Chanel knowledge, and has given numerous lectures on the history and fashions of Coco Chanel to her peers as well as to aspiring young girls.

As a member of The Executives' Wives' Cookbook Committee, Mrs. Christina Pebbleworth-Stafford's knowledge of French cuisine is invaluable. They are honored to have this individual with her important stature contribute to their project and causes.

MRS. CHRISTINA PEBBLEWORTH-STAFFORD'S CITRON PRESSE FOR THE LAWNBOY

1 lemon,
¼ cup very fine sugar
Perrier water
ice cubes

Squeeze the lemon in a lemon press. Put the juice in a tall glass. Sprinkle the sugar over the juice, and stir in the water. Add ice cubes.

Mrs. Christina Pebbleworth-Stafford was a very reserved, intelligent lady who made The Lawnboy nervous with her intimidating silences. He knew she expected him to work hard and smart.

She always had lemonade for him, and served it in a formal way. She always presented the lemonade on a silver tray with a linen napkin. She would invariably look at him with her dark eyes and say, "I know this doesn't taste like your usual lemonade, but it's how they make it in France."

He didn't think it tasted any different than other lemonade, but he had manners and thanked her, none the less.

---

[21] *Although the C major scale has no accidentals, i.e. sharps or flats; Christina's C scale does, unfortunately, contain two accidental sharps. They are called 'cold' sharp, and 'curt' sharp.*

[22] *She has some pretty impressive 'Rothchild blood' on her mother's side. Rumor has it that her father, because of his attitude, was kicked out of the Cordon Bleu Cooking School.*

BUNNY BAXLEY

BUNNY BAXLEY

To those who really know her, Bunny Baxley can be accurately described as a lady of show and a lady on the go. Because Bunny Baxley has looks and habits that can intimidate the best and brightest, she has some enemies. One of them, to most people's horror, once openly described her as a loose cannon with high heels and low morals.[23]

Bunny didn't let anyone's perception of her stand in her way. Even though she was observed kicking off her coral shoes to dance on a coffee table with a lit Pall Mall in one hand, and a Cosmopolitan in the other, she secretly enjoys watching other peoples' reactions to her seemingly outrageous behavior. She knows she's in charge. Her stunning confessions would be enough to send normal people to the 'couch man', but not Bunny Baxley. She's a mite of a person, but she's tough, and she knows how to survive anything, thanks to her early childhood.

Her childhood was not one that is usual for the social circle she now enjoys. For the first four years of her life, she was an orphan. By sure fate, a 'Daddy Warbucks' type and his prominent wife adopted this little, spit-fire red-head whom he endearingly called his 'Annie'.[24] This couple was totally smitten by and devoted to Bunny. They raised her in a life of privilege, money and notoriety. She was a natural. Her looks and her charm won over everyone until the 'nature over nurture' genes took over when her teen-age hormones kicked in with full force. Her parents were ready to give up, that is, until she met and married Johnny Baxley, a successful lawyer.

Johnny Baxley has the reputation of being smart, driven, and one who works under the table when needed. He has the uncanny ability to untangle people out of 'real messes'. He fell head over heels for Bunny, because she could hold her own with her friends, his friends, and her drinks. She never vied for attention, she just got it. Most importantly he has always appreciated the fact that she has never thought to question his business practices.

Besides Johnny, Bunny's world consists of many passions. This fashion icon loves couture, compacts, candlelight, carats, capsules, *carte blanc*, cashbooks, caterers, chain-smoking, chivalry, Christmas, codeine, country clubs and poodles -especially *Fifi*.[25] Bunny Baxley never learned to cook very well, but she loves to entertain and be entertained. She volunteers in her social circle, but because she gets easily distracted, she can't always be counted on to finish the task at hand. Her big contribution to The Executives' Wives' Cookbook Committee was her amazing knowledge of cocktails, and her willingness to co-chair the La La La La Lipstick Charity Ball.

BUNNY BAXLEY'S QUICK AND EASY LEMONADE FOR THE LAWNBOY

1 12 ounce can of frozen lemonade
3 cups of water
½ small bag of ice cubes

Take the can of frozen lemonade out of the freezer and let it thaw in the sink, or run hot water over the can. When the can feels soft (about 2 hours), open it with an electric can opener. Add 3 cups of water and stir with a large glass swizzle stick. Add the ice cubes and serve.

Bunny Baxley always had the ingredients for her lemonade recipe on hand. She appreciated the fact that The Lawnboy was not only good looking, strong and muscular, but that he was also willing to help her open the can of lemonade if she couldn't get her can opener to work properly. One time when The Lawnboy was at her house mowing, she looked at him, and inappropriately slurred, "How bout I add a little punch to that lemon?"

On hot, exhausting days, she would fix this lemonade recipe for her and her husband, Johnny. She would embellish it by adding three ounces of vodka to each glass.

---

[23] *Everyone on The Executives' Wives' Cookbook Committee knew that the 'One of them' referred to was Maribelle Biche so we're not telling you anything everybody doesn't know anyway. Like Bunny Baxley said to her dearest friend, Beebe Hall, "Consider the source. I have got so much on that lady, I could run her out of town, and Johnny has reassured me he has ways to even up the score. So there."*

[24] *Her adoptive dad let her sip from his cocktails at an early age.*

[25] *Her beloved poodle, Fifi, died of liver failure. It was the only time that Bunny Baxley's family and friends worried about her ability to cope with life. She wrote Judith Leiber to see if she would make a poodle purse for her. A customer service representative from Judith Leiber's company wrote back and said it was on the drawing board for sometime in the future.*

DORIS DUPRÉ

44

DORIS DUPRÉ

Prologue: In order to understand Doris Dupré, one of the ladies of The Executives' Wives' Cookbook Committee, one needs to be privy to some background information about this highly 'uspicioussay' kleptomaniac bunny 'illerkay.' Doris' bizarre childhood started in France where . .

Her father, a noted French aerial contortionist, and her mother an aerial ballerina/tightrope walker always appeared to fly through the air with the greatest of ease, but looks can be deceiving, especially in the make-believe world of the circus, and the 'tightrope' wasn't always so secure, and one day it snapped.

On that fateful day, Doris' mother and father, who were avid Monopoly players who played with their feet so as to enhance their flexibility, were immersed in an intense game that Doris' mother was losing. She had mortgaged all her properties to buy hotels on both Marvin Gardens and Boardwalk, and was down to $10.00. As luck *didn't* have it, she landed on "Chance," and was ordered to pay $15.00 poor tax. She said to her husband, the contortionist, "I'm not paying it. I've given more than my share of money to the poor. It's about time they started to fend for themselves." As it turned out, that was the wrong thing for her to say to her husband who was hurting because he was not only suffering from back spasms and a pulled groin, but an ingrown toenail too. Boldly cracking every knuckle on his fingers and toes (except the ingrown one) in her face, he glared at her, contorted his body, and yelled, "I've bent over backwards for you long enough! You're not going to wiggle out of this one. You either pay up, or," "Or what?" she yelled back, "Or drop dead," he sneered as he grabbed his suspenders, ballet shoes and tights to get ready for their next performance.

A few minutes after this episode, they were high up in the sky performing, as what turned out to be, their last aerial act. As he was about to throw her in the air and catch her with one hand tied behind his back, he supposedly whispered to her, "I'm about to see a fallen star." With that, she fell through the air and landed on the back of an elephant. The elephant threw her up in the air again with his trunk and she landed on the ground. She didn't die, but had massive head injuries, and slid into a permanent coma. Doris' father was kicked out of the circus for premeditated, suspicious behavior.

So he left. He packed up Doris, his comatose wife, and they joined the carnival. To earn some money, he put his wife in a wheel-chaired pram, billed her as 'the world's biggest baby who still takes a bottle,' and put her on for display for 75 cents a look. He ordered Doris to stand by her mother, hold a bottle in her mouth, take it out and replace it with a teething ring or pacifier, and watch her closely so she didn't choke. He smooth-talked the bearded lady into handling the details and to make sure the act looked authentic. In the meantime he took up with the lady who had the world's smallest waist. He entertained himself by helping her cinch and lace her corset.

After about a month of carnival life, Doris' mother expired. Some of the carnival people tried to take her under their wings by befriending her. The bearded lady taught her how to cheat at Dominos and shave her upper lip. The lead midway barker taught her how to shoot at plastic ducks so that they would tip over in the water. The magician taught her how to make bunnies disappear in black, top hats and the carnival's money handler taught her how to talk and do business in Pig Latin. The cotton candy lady let her sleep under her cart when Doris' dad wasn't around because he was too busy cinching up the lady with the world's smallest waist.

In her spare time Doris fantasized about finding Big Foot and Martians. She loved to read <u>Ripley's Believe it or Not</u> cartoons, and dreamed about having a farm as big as Beatrix Potter's, a place where she could plant massive flower and vegetable gardens and shoot rabbits out of Mr. McGregor's garden.

Her life took a radical turn when the carnival palmistry reader read her palms and told her she had earth hands; her fate line indicated she would be a socially, connected horticulturist who' illedkay unniesbay' and a distant relative would change her life and his reading came true.

Her mother's sister, a New York socialite who read about her sister's unfortunate demise, sought out Doris and found her. She took her back to New York, cleaned her up, and sent her to Cornell University to study. At Cornell, Doris, much to the consternation of her socialite aunt, majored in horticulture. It was in the horticultural lab, where she met her husband, 'logKay upres'Day' a trust-funded [26] scientist who often times spoke like her in 'igPay atinLay', and who was devoted to finding ways to keep 'abbitsray omfray eatingay uliptays'.

They quickly married and bought massive amounts of property which they turned into lavish gardens. They hosted elaborate parties, and soon they became the envy of everyone in a 300 mile radius. Because they appeared to be wealthy and prosperous, and because many on The Executives' Wives' Cookbook Committee wanted to be invited to the Dupré's parties, they asked her to join their committee. She agreed to join because, for once in her life, she wanted to at least appear as if she were normal. However, her past began to dictate who she was, and everyone soon found out she was 'arfay omfray ormalnay'.

Shortly after she hosted her party, Doris Dupré left The Executives' Wives' Cookbook Committee. It was *Abracadabra* for the Duprés. Everyone was relieved, but they still envied her country estate, her gardens, and her obvious monetary means.

DORIS DUPRÉ'S SECRET LEMONADE RECIPE FOR THE LAWNBOY

Doris Dupré was a secretive lady who had an expansive lawn, massive lush gardens, and a staff for all of it. Before he was hired, The Lawnboy was instructed on her long list of don'ts. These rules consisted of: Don't talk to other employees about anything but work; don't tell others that don't work here about my rules; and remember, don't tell anyone I smoke. When you're done, knock four times on my door, and I will know it is you. The Lawnboy thought her rules were odd, but she always had lemonade ready for him, and she paid him well.

Note: Doris refused to give anyone her lemonade recipe.

---

[26] *Klog Dupré's family made their money on cultivating the famous Semper Augustus tulip bulb. When the tulip bulb bubble burst, they hid out in the 'illshay' of anceFray' and started 'armingfay'. To insure anonymity and keep their enemies at bay, the family changed their name from Van De Pré to 'uprésDay' and spoke in 'igPay atinLay'. The family moved to the United States and kept a low profile for generations.*

MARIBELLE BICHE

MARIBELLE BICHE

The 'many-mooded' Maribelle Biche came from a stolid, cold-climate family. After she graduated with honors from Bennington, she had two serious suitors; Robert Biche and John Carin, - who coincidentally were finishing Yale Law School at the same time. She chose to marry Robert Biche because he was offered a job in a more prestigious law firm than John, and his family had more money.

Even though marriage is not about love for Maribelle, but about a team to look good, she is calculating enough to know she can make it work. Besides, they have some things in common. They both like money and they both have a hard time parting with 'a buck', especially when it comes to tipping people. It surprises no one how they complain about the difficulty in keeping good help.

Robert Biche likes good food, and she has always been a marvelous cook. Robert wanted a lady who acted independent, could hold her own and not be intimidated by anyone or anything. Maribelle fits the bill. Like him, Maribelle is egotistical, opinionated, arbitrary, reserved, forbidding, demanding of herself and others and more often than not, cold-hearted.

When he married her, Robert knew that Maribelle was quarrelsome, temperamental, cold and easily miffed. Like a good lawyer, he has learned when to fight, and when to give up fighting.

The Executives' Wives' Cookbook Committee accepts her because she is a genius when it comes to mastering cooking and understanding fine cuisine. They know there is no one better than her at her craft; and that is why they understand that they must make allowances for this lady who won't tolerate idle chatter, won't take no for an answer and won't settle for anything less than complete perfection.

MARIBELLE BICHE'S
NO LEMONADE FOR THE LAWNBOY

As usual, when The Lawnboy went to Maribelle Biche's home, she wasn't home.

As usual, he would go around her house, ringing her doorbells until he came to one of her doors that had a note attached to it which read: "I'm not home. Mow the lawn, shut the garage door when you're done, and I will pay you next time you come. Have a nice day. Maribelle"

As usual, he quenched his thirst on rusty water from the hose because, as usual, there was no 'Lemonade for The Lawnboy.'

PART II

THE COOKBOOK

Mrs. Jonathan Hurlinger's Menu

Cocktails

Appetizer
CRAB MEAT FROMAGE

Soup
BOULA BOULA

Main Course
J. EDGAR HOOVER'S POPOVERS

FRENCH CARROTS

SAFFRON RICE

CHÂTEAUBRIAND

BEAUJOLAIS

Dessert
CRÈME BRÛLÉE

After Dinner
COFFEE
COGNAC

MRS. JONATHAN HURLINGER'S KICK-OFF DINNER FOR THE MEMBERS OF THE EXECUTIVES' WIVES' COOKBOOK COMMITTEE.

As the newly elected president of the The Executives' Wives' Cookbook Committee, the most capable and brilliant Mrs. Jonathan Hurlinger, in all her elegance and passions in indulging in the pleasure of entertaining, invites The Executives' Wives' Cookbook Committee to her beautiful and luxurious home for a kick-off dinner. She hired Pierre, supposedly a most-noted French chef, to test her recipes, cook and present the dinner, and answer questions from the ladies of The Executives' Wives' Cookbook Committee.

In not wanting to cut corners, Mrs. Jonathan Hurlinger hired Pierre to set the stage and raise the bar. Her goal was to see that the cookbook would be such a grand culinary masterpiece, that every other charitable committee would be envious of the importance, significance, and success of the members of The Executives' Wives' Cookbook Committee. By setting the standards high, Mrs. Jonathan Hurlinger knew that it was a guarantee that everyone would talk about The Executives' Wives' Cookbook Committee's herculean undertaking for years to come.

Mrs. Jonathan Hurlinger had gone to great lengths to be well-prepared and organized for the kick-off dinner she was hosting. She hired The Lawnboy to help both her and Pierre. She organized and selected the committee assignments, and had even suggested types of luncheons and/or dinners that would be suitable for each individual lady to host. She convinced Pierre to let each of the ladies ask him a question concerning French food, or a question on the fine art of cooking, while they were watching him prepare the dinner.

The only things she wasn't prepared for were the actions and reactions of the ladies, and this was where things got out of control, and Mrs. Jonathan Hurlinger's plans for the evening started to break down.

In hindsight, she realized her mistakes were two-fold. To begin with, she had allocated too much time for cocktails. Because of this, most of the ladies were tipsy, and the questions they asked of the French chef were beyond embarrassment for both Pierre and Mrs. Jonathan Hurlinger, and allowing questions was her second mistake.

Pierre wasn't prepared for the questions, and the faux pas went from bad to worse. Most of the questions he ignored, but since the ladies weren't paying attention, the only one who felt uncomfortable was Mrs. Jonathan Hurlinger. Pierre just looked terribly annoyed.

It was bad enough when Beebe Hall asked him if he had ever singed his eyelashes while flaming, and Bunny Baxley asked him if he liked poodles, but when Mrs. Grant Goldman-Hues asked him if he had ever met Coco Chanel, and Mrs. Stanley Bigsbee started talking inappropriately about him, *Moulin Rouge*, lipstick and The Lawnboy, he whispered to Mrs. Jonathan Hurlinger that he might leave. She discreetly convinced him to stay. He felt sorry for her, so he did stay, but things got worse.

Mrs. Charles Chatterton asked him what the French ladies ate or didn't eat to stay so thin, and Doris Dupré asked him if he would reveal French rabbit recipes for both *Champagne D'Argent* rabbits and French Lop rabbits. At this point, Katrina Canfield, not wanting to miss a golden opportunity to let Doris know that she knew about her bunny secrets, chimed in and asked Pierre, "Is there such a thing as a rabbit punch?" Maribelle Biche, not understanding the dynamics between Doris Dupré and Katrina Canfield, heard the word 'recipe' and boldly asked Pierre if he would be so kind as to give her all his recipes. If that wasn't enough, Mrs. Samuel Squire asked him if his family coat of arms was historically honorable, and Mrs. Elmer Steele tactlessly and boldly told him that many of his French recipes were really English. He had all he could do to contain himself. He was livid!

He knew that when Mrs. Christina Pebbleworth-Stafford asked him her question in fluent French, she didn't care about his answer, but she was only trying to impress him and the other ladies. Likewise, when Katrina Canfield tried to impress him and her cohorts with her knowledge of noted French chefs, and which restaurants had what Michelin star rating, he knew what she was doing too.

The straw that broke the camel's back came when Mrs. Molly McCurdle asked him what he thought French fairy princesses would eat in the 21st century. Thank goodness for Mrs. Jonathan Hurlinger, who had just finished preparing the food, because it was obvious he couldn't take any more. He glared at the ladies and said, "I feel like I am in an American junior high home economics class where you are all learning how to broil grapefruit that you have sectioned and covered in brown sugar." After having said that, he left.

Mrs. Jonathan Hurlinger was visibly shaken as was Martha Payne who hadn't dared ask the chef anything. Mrs. Michael Stellar and Mrs. E.O.Bittleduke were watching what was unfolding, and with their good manners they had opted not to say anything.

Mrs. Jonathan Hurlinger knew she had to act 'presidential' because she was their president. In her most professional way, she addressed the ladies, who by now had no clue what was going on. She boldly, with much chagrin, said that chefs who are creative geniuses are sometimes temperamental, have big egos and are not used to random chatter outside their realm.

She asked The Lawnboy to take over and serve the meal, and he agreed. She knew he would graciously handle the ladies. He had done it before, he could do anything, he looked so handsome and he was a pro at it.

After it was all over, and The Lawnboy was cleaning up, even he was relieved that Pierre, the chef, had gone. The Lawnboy knew there was no way that Pierre could idly sit back and watch Doris Dupré shove food in her pockets and Mrs. Elmer Steele shove food in her mouth. The Lawnboy knew Pierre would be offended by watching the ladies play with their food rather than eat it. He knew it would be somewhat offensive for Pierre to hear the ladies talk about their inappropriate escapades in Paris, but really offensive to hear Bunny Baxley, in her sing-song voice, giggle and say, "*Pardonnez-Moi*, can I ask for a doggy bag for Fifi?"

Crab Meat *Fromage*

½ cup butter
1 small onion, minced
¼ cup flour
1 teaspoon salt
⅛ teaspoon white pepper
2 cups half and half
2 cans crab meat (6 ½ ounces), drained
16 strips cheddar cheese
½ cup bread crumbs, buttered

In a large saucepan, melt butter. Add onion, and cook until onion is opaque. Gradually stir in the flour, salt, white pepper and half and half. Cook until thickened. Break the crab meat into small chunks and put it in the mixture. Spoon the crab meat mixture into buttered, individual, crab shells. Put a strip of the cheddar cheese on each shell and sprinkle with crumbs. Bake at 450° for 10-15 minutes, or until the cheese is melted and the crumbs are slightly browned.

Some of the ladies didn't even try to eat the appetizer. Mrs. Elmer Steele downed two of them in 15 minutes. Mrs. Charles Chatterton timed her.

Boula-Boula

4 cups peas, cleaned and shelled

3 tablespoons butter
1 teaspoon salt
1 teaspoon white pepper
2 cups sherry
4 cups canned, green, turtle soup

1 cup whipping cream

Cook the peas in boiling water until they are soft. Drain the peas and purée them. Put the puréed peas back into a kettle and add the butter, salt and pepper. Pour in the sherry and turtle soup. Heat, but don't boil. Pour the soup into bowls and top with a dollop of whipped cream.

According to Mrs. Jonathan Hurlinger, this was one of Jackie Kennedy's soup recipes. Pierre thought the soup recipe was a good choice because Jackie Kennedy liked the French people, and she wasn't a cowgirl. All the ladies tried it because they all thought Jackie Kennedy had lots of style in both couture and cuisine choices. Nobody finished it.

J. Edgar Hoover's Popovers

6 eggs
½ teaspoon salt
1 teaspoon sugar
2 cups flour
2 cups milk
4 tablespoons butter, melted

With an electric mixer beat the eggs until they are frothy. Add salt, sugar, flour, half the milk and mix until the batter is smooth. Add the remaining milk and melted butter, until mixture is blended. Pour the batter into hot, popover pans, filling each about half full. Bake at 450° for 15 minutes. Reduce oven heat to 375° and continue baking for 15 minutes longer. When the popovers are brown and crisp, remove from cups by turning upside down. Place hot popover on a bread and butter plate and serve immediately to guests who are already seated at the table.

Note: Before adding the popover mixture, preheat empty buttered, muffin (if using muffin tins) tins to 450° and heat them until they are sizzling.

Doris Dupré wouldn't eat the popovers because she thought she was on one of J. Edgar's 'hit lists.' Just to make a point, Mrs. Samuel Squire, boldly ate two of them.

French Carrots

4 cups fresh carrots, cut into 3 inch long
matchstick strips
¼ cup orange juice, unsweetened
4 tablespoons sugar
½ cup butter
1 teaspoon salt
½ teaspoon pepper

dill weed, dried

Parboil carrots in a large saucepan. Drain water and
melt butter in the same saucepan. Add carrots and
sprinkle with sugar, salt and pepper. Simmer until
carrots are tender and have a syrup glaze covering
them. Sprinkle them with dried dill weed and serve in
a warmed bowl.

*Bunny Baxley told everyone she ate carrots to improve her
vision. She said, "Once I was pulled over on a highway by
a policeman who said I was weaving. I told him my vision
was impaired that day because I had forgotten to eat my
carrots. He felt sorry for me and he let me go. Johnny said
the policeman owed him a favor, and that's why I didn't get
a ticket. I don't know who to believe."*

Saffron Rice

2 cups white rice, uncooked
4 cups chicken broth

½ teaspoon saffron, softened in hot water
and crumbled
4 tablespoons butter
1 onion, chopped
1 teaspoon salt

Bring chicken broth to a boil. Add the saffron, butter,
onion and salt. Wash the rice and put it in a baking
dish. Pour the chicken broth mixture over it and bake
at 375° for 40 minutes.

*Rice was always a hit with the ladies because it was
considered a 'diet' food.*

Châteaubriand

6 pounds whole beef tenderloin
1 cup sweet white wine
½ cup brandy
½ teaspoon thyme
1 teaspoon salt
¼ teaspoon pepper
1 bay leaf
1 small onion

1 pound fresh mushrooms, thinly sliced
½ cup butter

parsley

The day before serving, place the beef in a large
container and sprinkle with wine. Cover and marinate
for 24 hours, turning occasionally.

The next day, preheat the oven to 450°. Melt butter.
Stir in brandy, thyme, salt, pepper, and bay leaf. Add
onion and simmer until liquid is reduced by half. Add
mushrooms and simmer for 4 minutes.

Remove beef from marinade and reserve marinade for
basting.

Cut a pocket lengthwise in the beef. Fill it with
mushroom mixture, and skewer the opening. Roast in
a preheated oven for 45 minutes (rare), to 1 ½ hours
for (well-done). Baste frequently with pan juices and
reserved marinade. If the beef appears to be getting
too brown, tent it with a large piece of tin foil. Cut
into 1 inch pieces and serve on a heated platter that
has been decorated with snippets of parsley.

Bearnaise Sauce

4 egg yolks
3 tablespoons lemon juice
1 ½ tablespoons dry white wine
½ tablespoon, Balsamic vinegar
1 cup cold butter
2 tablespoons of fresh tarragon

In a small saucepan, stir the egg yolks, lemon juice, white wine and Balsamic vinegar. Add ½ cup of butter. Stir over very low heat until the butter is melted. Add another ½ cup of cold butter. Continue stirring until butter is melted and sauce thickened. Add 2 tablespoons of fresh tarragon. Serve hot as an accompaniment to the beef steaks.

Note: This is an easy *Bearnaise* sauce which requires little skill.

Someone saw Doris Dupré take some of the beef, put it in a container and quickly shove it in her handbag. Bunny Baxley heard about it and said to Beebe Hall, "If Doris Dupré is that desperate, maybe she should be our worthy cause."

Crème Brûlée

1 quart heavy cream
12 egg yolks
1 cup sugar
1 teaspoon salt
4 teaspoons vanilla

1 cup brown sugar

Place twelve custard cups in large roasting pan. Pour the cream into a saucepan and heat until the boiling point. Beat the egg yolks, sugar and salt. Pour the hot cream over the egg yolk mixture. Add vanilla, and continue to stir. Pour the custard into the custard cups. Pour enough hot water into the roasting pan to come halfway up the sides of the cups. Bake at 350° for about 35 minutes, or until the custards are set in the center. Remove from water, cool and chill overnight.

Preheat broiler. Arrange custard cups on a baking sheet. Sprinkle 1 teaspoon brown sugar over each. Broil until sugar browns, rotating baking sheet for even browning for about 2 minutes. Chill custards at least one hour before serving.

Even though their mouths were watering, the ladies who didn't like caloric-laden dishes said "No thank you" when they were offered the Crème Brûlée.

BEEBE HALL'S GEORGE WASHINGTON PARTY
AND HER INFAMOUS CHERRIES JUBILEE

Beebe Hall was famous for entertaining with fire and alcohol, and entertained to celebrate any time there was an excuse to celebrate. Beebe Hall made a Cherries Jubilee dessert when she was hosting a dinner party to try out some of her recipes for The Executives' Wives' Cookbook, and, of course, to celebrate George Washington's birthday. She put a lot of thought and hard work into this dinner party. She even went so far as to have trusted an engraver/calligrapher to hand-draw cherry trees on each of the name cards. Her dinner guests included just a few of her friends who weren't in Naples at this time of the year. They were: Dr. E.O. Bittleduke, Beebe Hall's retired gynecologist, and his wife, Barbara, who was the ultimate embodiment of cautious restraint, Mr. and Mrs. Samuel Squire, a local successful developer and his wife, Dorothy, who were both bona fide members of numerous exclusive and impressive historical associations such as the Society of the Washington Family Descendants, various Mt. Vernon societies, Sons and Daughters of the American Revolution, and, of course, Johnny and Bunny Baxley, who were always invited.

As Beebe Hall recalled, the dinner conversation was quite boring, with Mr. Samuel Squire dominating the conversation about who was really pedigreed, who thought he should be, and who really wasn't. Johnny Baxley smirked to himself when he saw how his wife perked up when she heard the word 'pedigree' and started to talk about her poodle, Fifi, and her impressive blood lines. She explained that Fifi was no ordinary poodle, but a descendant of Jacqueline Susann's beloved poodle, Josephine's friskiest playmate, Coco, who, she continued, was named after Coco Chanel. Mr. Samuel Squire, at this time, cleared his throat and squirmed because he had no idea what and who Bunny was talking about, and didn't consider it relevant. Mrs. Samuel Squire, who was notably uncomfortable and nervous for both of them, secretly hoped the conversation and atmosphere would change instantly, and she knew the ball was in her court. Picking up her glass, she hurriedly downed her Cosmopolitan. With uncharacteristic boldness, Mrs. Samuel Squire started talking about the variety of

cherry trees at Mt. Vernon, and how she was consulted, in addition to advising, the head horticulturist at Mt. Vernon, as to what varieties of cherry trees needed to be planted, and more importantly, where they should plant them. Bunny Baxley who wasn't really following the conversation at all, picked up her place card and commented on how the calligrapher should have drawn the cherry tree 'chopped down'. Mrs. Samuel Squire, still acting boldly, was just starting to inform Bunny Baxley, and anyone else who would listen, that it was common knowledge that George really didn't chop down a cherry tree. As she was planning to further expound upon the George Washington cherry tree myth, Beebe Hall, with a grand and impressive entrance, came into the dining room with her famous flaming Cherries Jubilee dessert, and proudly placed it on the tea cart for everyone to admire.

Mrs. E. O. Bittleduke, who up to this point was preoccupied with watching how her husband, Dr. E. O. Bittleduke, was responding to the idle chatter at the table, 'goggled' over the Cherries Jubilee and told Beebe Hall she just knew it would taste as wonderful as it looked. She had no sooner said that, when her retired gynecologist husband, Dr. E.O. Bittleduke, who had been recently diagnosed with early stages of forgetfulness and wasn't included in a lot of intimate dinner parties, and due to his condition hadn't 'wintered' for the past two years, started talking inappropriately in 'gynecology terminology'. Beebe Hall who wasn't known to let anything shock her, blushed and turned as red as the flames on her dessert. Jimmy, Beebe Hall's husband winked at her and whispered "Are you having an episode?"

At this point, Bunny Baxley was about to break out in laughter. She covered her mouth with her damask napkin and stained the cloth with her new Lancôme cherry/merlôt lipstick she was wearing and had purchased especially for this occasion. Beebe Hall, desperately pretended that nothing happened and quickly dished up Cherries Jubilee for everyone.

Mrs. Samuel Squire, who at this point was so uncomfortable she wanted to leave, started to choke and turned red as a cherry. Bunny Baxley, who always watched everything and everybody yelled, "Is there a doctor in the house?" Dr. E.O. Bittleduke, looked up, took out his billfold and started passing his cards around. Johnny, Bunny Baxley's husband, who was a pro at acting quickly when a crisis arose, jumped up and, as appropriately as he could, smacked Mrs. Samuel Squire on her upper back. The force of the blow caused Mrs. Samuel Squire to open her mouth and the cherry pit projected through the air. It flew through the 2nd and 3rd candles of the candelabra, and made a perfect landing on Mr. Samuel Squire's lapel flag pin which he had personally received from Henry Cabot Lodge Jr. at the 1960 Republican Convention in San Francisco. In desperation, Mrs. Samuel Squire, excused herself, picked up her handbag and went to the ladies' room. Mrs. E. O. Bittleduke, feeling equally as desperate, and knowing she had some little pills in her purse that would help both of them, followed her.

With Mrs. Samuel Squire and Mrs. E.O. Bittleduke off in the ladies' room, Beebe Hall settled down, but only for a moment. Bunny Baxley, who was only interested in the brandy sauce on the dessert, gently and as inconspicuously as she could, pushed her dessert aside, but it ended right next to Dr. E.O. Bittleduke's plate. Practicing his most recent habit, Dr. E.O. Bittleduke temporarily forgot what he was doing and started eating Bunny Baxley's dessert. In his confusion his sport jacket sleeve, shirt cuff and Pierre Cardin monogrammed 'B'cufflinks landed in the dessert. The white damask table cloth became awash in cherry juice, cherries, and two, bright red 'B' cufflink marks. Bunny Baxley, not wanting to embarrass Dr. E.O. Bittleduke, tried to smooth things over and make light of the incident by saying, "Oh, Dr. Bittleduke, look at those two Bs on the tablecloth. I bet that stands for Bebee and Bunny, your two favorite former patients." Before Dr. E.O. Bittleduke could attempt to figure out what Bunny Baxley was talking about, Mrs. E.O. Bittleduke and Mrs. Samuel Squire returned from the ladies' room. They quickly announced it was time to leave and graciously thanked the Halls for the wonderful time. Bunny and Johnny Baxley stayed to drink some more Cosmopolitans and talk about, as Beebe Hall said, 'my most inappropriate' dinner party.

When Beebe Hall's dry cleaner apologized for not getting the stains out, Beebe Hall wasn't upset. As she later told Bunny Baxley, "that whole party was a permanent blot." Bunny Baxley laughed, and replied, "You mean a bloody mess."

Cherries Jubilee

2 pounds Bing cherries, pitted
1 cup sugar
⅛ teaspoon salt
2 tablespoons cornstarch
1 ½ cups water
2 pints vanilla ice cream
¼ cup brandy
square, toasted bread cubes

Combine the sugar, salt, cornstarch and water. Add
the pitted cherries and cook until thickened, stirring
constantly. Soak bread squares in brandy. Scoop very
hard, vanilla ice cream into individual, dessert cups.
Pour jubilee mixture over ice cream, place brandied
bread on top, ignite and serve.

61

MRS. BEEBE HALL'S FLAMING FLAMBÉ FIASCO

COCKTAILS
Flaming Absinthe
Flaming Sambuca

SOUP
Flaming Onion Soup

SALAD
Flaming Spinach Salad

MAIN COURSE
Brussel Sprouts
Volcanic Sweet Potatoes
Steak Flambé

DESSERT
Flaming Peaches

AFTER DINNER COCKTAIL
Café Brulôt

BEEBE HALL'S FLAMBÉ DINNER PARTY

Beebe Hall was excited that The Executives' Wives' Cookbook Committee unanimously voted her to be in charge of all the flambé recipes for the cookbook, even though it caused her some embarrassment. When the vote came in 'unanimously' everyone knew Beebe Hall had voted for herself. Her best friend, Bunny Baxley, told her, "Not to worry. Nobody can hold a candle to you, when it comes to smoke and fire, and everyone knows it."

Beebe Hall decided that she would host The Executives' Wives' Cookbook Committee for a flamboyant, flambé, fun-filled, festive, dinner party and try to 'flame-up' the recipes she was going to put in the cookbook. She had good intentions of hosting this dinner on George Washington's birthday, and she tried. However, most of the committee members were 'wintering' on George's birthday. She, being the lightning ball she is, threw another party. She didn't invite the executive wives' husbands because, as she said to her husband, "I want to get this cookbook committee fired up, and I can't be distracted by having some of the men douse the flames, fire and fun." [27]

She knew it was a given that Martha Payne, with her frightful aversion to smoke, fire and ice wouldn't come, and she was right. That was just fine with Beebe Hall. She couldn't understand Martha Payne's problems anyway. As she said to her friend, Bunny Baxley, "Someone needs to put a cherry bomb under her and scare the living daylights right out of her. It would give Miss Payne something to shake about."

Mrs. Samuel Squire couldn't make it because she and her husband were off at another Republican convention. "Just as well," Bunny Baxley said.

She was surprised and somewhat annoyed that Mrs. Christina Pebbleworth-Stafford wasn't going to come, but Bunny Baxley told her she knew the reason. She said, "Last week when I called Johnsons to get some more scotch delivered, the new clerk told me that she had overheard Mrs. Christina Pebbleworth-Stafford

tell Mrs. Jonathan Hurlinger that she couldn't bear to go because everything about Beebe Hall including her house always smells of smoke, and she wasn't willing to have her clothes ruined, and she wasn't willing to compromise her fashion forté or her high standards by wearing just any old thing." She continued, "Not to worry Beebe, you wouldn't want people at your home that won't loosen up, light up or live it up!"

Mrs. Elmer Steele called Beebe Hall and told her that she was coming, but, as she told Mrs. Michael Stellar, "I'm only going because I need to sample the recipes, and for that reason only. That house is a fire hazard. Just look at her singed arms and eyebrows. That wasn't done by her esthetician."

Everyone else on The Executives' Wives' Cookbook Committee, including Doris Dupré, was looking forward to the event. The party was not billed as a 'theme event', but everybody knew what everyone would do, so, of course, they all dressed for show. Molly McCurdle, in keeping with the spirit of the party, wore a wispy, red, sheer, organza wrap over her floral, spaghetti, strap dress. Her wrap was anchored by a diamond/ruby-encrusted firefly-in-motion-brooch. Mrs. Michael Stellar told her it was beautiful, but the rest of the ladies didn't say anything. They all thought she looked way too 'fu fu' and flighty.

Both Mrs. Stanley Bigsbee and Mrs. Charles Chatterton (Charlotte & Charlotte) came dressed in striking but similar red, linen sheaths and red and white, spectator pumps. They both carried Louis Vitton clutches filled with pills and powder, lipstick and lighters, cash and compacts and, of course, Old Gold cigarettes. Mrs. Charles Chatterton's clutch was trimmed in a small band of mink and Mrs.Stanley Bigsbee's clutch was topped off with a red, crystal clasp. They looked like the Bobbsie Twins, but they liked it that way. With fire-engine red lipstick on their lips, a little bit outside the lip line, and scarlet-red, shiny, fingernail polish lacquered on perfectly manicured fingernails, they looked like, as Bunny

---

[27] *After her George Washington party, Beebe Hall didn't want to be bothered thinking about Dr. E.O. Bittleduke wandering around getting burned and saying inappropriate things. She also didn't want to have to put up with Mr. Samuel Squire and his boring ramblings.*

Baxley whispered to Beebe Hall, "Ripe, ready and revved up for the fire."

Maribelle Biche was horrified that both she and Mrs. Jonathan Hurlinger were also carrying matching red Louis Vitton bags. Mrs. Jonathan Hurlinger took it all in stride, but it was obvious by the way she pouted that it totally wrecked Maribelle Biche's evening.

Everyone noticed that Mrs. Elmer Steele was really showing her age. They were all a little concerned, but mostly curious as to why she had let herself go so badly. Dressed in a white blouse, red pleated skirt and red blazer,[28] she looked like she was going to her funeral. Mrs. Charles Chatterton whispered to Mrs. Stanley Bigsbee (of course, everyone within 10 feet of them heard her), "Oh, the poor lady, she looks like a round, squishy over-ripe tomato well past her due date. The only firm thing about her is her mind." A giggling Mrs. Stanley Bigsbee put her finger over her lips and whispered back to Mrs. Charles Chatterton, "Hush, hush, sweet Charlotte." Everyone within range heard it, and thought, "Oh, what a clever lady that Mrs. Stanley Bigsbee can be, even in her questionable state."

Mrs. Grant Goldman-Hues came so bejeweled in garnets, rubies and diamonds, she looked frightfully gaudy. As Mrs. Jonathan Hurlinger whispered to Mrs. Michael Stellar, "Goodness, just look at her decked out in all her razzle-dazzle. She's lit up like a Merry Christmas tree. They should haul her out of here before someone goes blind."

Doris Dupré was, as usual, dressed smartly in clothes accented with suspiciously, over-sized pockets and garden flower motifs; and Katrina Canfield came dressed in her usual, expensive, contemporary, artsy, minimalist dress that only she could carry off in style.

As always, Mrs. Michael Stellar, and Mrs. E.O. Bittleduke looked lovely and refreshingly crisp in their summer linens. They looked as though they had walked out of the summer issue of a country club golfers' wives' magazine.

Bunny Baxley had come over at noon to help Beebe Hall get ready for the big event. Like teenagers, Bunny Baxley and Beebe Hall had primped all day, trying on one outfit after another. In between drinks and trying on different shades of lipstick and fingernail polish, they both finally settled on wearing outfits that were inappropriate, but eye-catching.

Beebe Hall was grateful for Bunny Baxley's help even though Beebe Hall was surprisingly well-organized. She had hired her florist to make centerpieces of a variety of red flowers, roman candles, black cats, sparklers, cherry bombs and other firecrackers. She told Bunny Baxley, "After the party's over, and everyone's gone, these centerpieces are going up in smoke and not without a big, bang boom!"

She had hired The Lawnboy and a caterer to make the food. She knew she would have to be in charge of the flames and the food preparation could distract her. Bunny Baxley reassured her that it was a smart move. As she said, "That's why God made caterers."

Beebe Hall put Bunny Baxley in charge of beverages and Bunny Baxley took over like a pro. When Beebe Hall was busy getting the sternos ready, Bunny Baxley called Johnsons and ordered another case of Ever Clear for the cherry bomb cocktails she was making. As she told Beebe Hall, "After looking at your stash of liquor, I ordered more Ever Clear, because we don't want to run out. My own personal recipe is a sure-fire winner. It reads like this, "Make them strong and it won't take long before the whole bloody group is 'over and out' bombed." And her recipe worked.

After several cocktails, most everyone was feeling quite tipsy as they made their way to the dining room to sit down to eat and watch the flambé show. Beebe was excited, but inebriated. As we all know, accidents do happen and they did. Like spontaneous combustion, everything erupted like a well-orchestrated volcanic disaster. It started with Mrs. Stanley Bigsbee. In her slurred voice she excused herself to go to the powder room. Mrs. Charles

---

[28] *She always wore a gold, jeweled lapel pin that had the letters 'PP' encircled with rubies on the face of the pin. PP stands for 'Past President,' and the pin stood for a host of organizations she presided over. Maribelle Biche says she knows firsthand that it wasn't a thank you gift from an organization she steered, but rather Mrs. Elmer Steele had it made for herself.*

Chatterton, who was sitting next to her and had just lit up an Old Gold, was helping Mrs. Stanley Bigsbee move her chair out when her cigarette fell out of her hand and into her lap and started to burn the fur on her Louis Vitton clutch. Mrs. Stanley Bigsbee staggered out of the dining room without knowing what just happened.

Mrs. Charles Chatterton, in a frenzied state tried to get her chair to slide back, but before she could catch her balance she and the chair fell over backwards and her smoldering clutch fell on the floor. Maribelle Biche grabbed the clutch, put it on her plate and poured water over it before she bent over to help Mrs. Charles Chatterton, whose spectator pumps' heels were caught in the second rung of the chair and whose body was in a 'sit-up' position. She didn't look too uncomfortable, even if her dress was half-way up her thighs. It was obvious she didn't feel too uncomfortable, because she was either passed out or in one of her narcoleptic states. Nevertheless, Mrs. E.O. Bittleduke tried to smooth the embarrassment over by saying, "Charlotte, are you practicing one of your water skiing maneuvers?" even though she clearly remembered what her husband's confidential medical files said about Mrs. Charles Chatterton's many-faceted problems.

As Maribelle Biche bent down to help Mrs. Charles Chatterton, she got too close to the steak *flambé* that Beebe Hall had just lit and set down in front of her. The fire from the steak *flambé*, jumped to Maribelle Biche's overly hair sprayed, coiffed hair-do. With the flames shooting up, she looked like the red devil from Dante's Inferno.[29] Maribelle Biche grabbed her handbag and started pounding out the flames with it. Beebe, whose husband Jimmy, an insurance man, always made sure there were plenty of fire extinguishers around, ran to get an extinguisher at the same time Bunny ran to get a bottle of water to pour on poor Maribelle Biche's coiffed hair-do. Instead, she grabbed the Ever Clear, and poured it over Maribelle Biche's hair-do, but, thankfully, Beebe Hall was right there with the fire extinguisher. Even though Maribelle Biche looked like a drowned, singed rat, she was okay and excused herself to go to the bathroom

when Mrs. Charles Chatterton woke up and mumbled incoherently about a cigarette.

Thinking she was going to reach her pack of Old Golds, Mrs. Charles Chatterton started pulling on the edge of the tablecloth which caused the candelabra to tip over. At this point, Maribelle Biche took off running for the bathroom, which caused her to miss seeing the fire from the tipped candelabra start the ends of Mrs. Molly McCurdle's red, organza wrap on fire. Mrs. Molly McCurdle jumped up, took off her wrap and started waving it around like a fire fly in distress, hoping the fire would go out. No such luck. The end of her smoldering wrap ignited the sparkler that was in a floral arrangement and it quickly started to sparkle and burn down.

When cool-headed Katrina Canfield saw what was going on, she grabbed the sparkler out of the floral arrangement, ran to the door, and yelled back, "I'm leaving; this is TTU."[30] Doris Dupré, who never did care for Katrina Canfield and her attitude, was feeling bold. She ran after her, sneered at her and said, "People who live in glass houses shouldn't throw sticks." Katrina Canfield, who wasn't used to being mocked, threw Doris Dupré the sparkler, and said, "Here's your stick, but I'm sure you meant stones." Doris Dupré, who was getting really agitated by now yelled back, "Sticks and stones may break my bones, but names will never kill me." Katrina Canfield had all she could take, and yelled back, "Names sure will kill you, bunny-killer." Doris Dupré, looking like she had just seen a dead rabbit, was horrified by now. Visibly shaken, she scurried into the house, quickly put the rest of the fireworks from the floral arrangement into her pockets, and left immediately.

As she was leaving, she bumped into Mrs. Elmer Steele who was leaving in a hurry and huff. Mrs. Elmer Steele, who had only come to taste the food, had burned her tongue on the steak *flambé*. She snorted as she said to Doris Dupré, "There are just no rules around here. I'm going to leave before it gets as out of control as Guy Fawkes[31] and the whole bloody place burns to the ground." Meanwhile, Mrs. Charles Chatterton was still on the floor in her water skiing

[29] *It was a Divine Comedy!*
[30] *Totally Torn Up*

65

position. They just left her there because Bunny Baxley placed a lit Old Gold in her mouth and seemed incoherent and comfortable. Besides, there were more immediate issues they had to take care of, and fast.

Mrs. Michael Stellar came running out of the bathroom yelling that Mrs. Stanley Bigsbee was passed out on the floor. The medicine cabinet was open and pills were all over the sink, and a few had fallen into the bidet. Mrs. Stanley Bigsbee's lipstick tube was opened and smeared all over her red sheath, pearls, front enameled teeth, and on the tile floor. Her compact was open, powder was everywhere, and the compact mirror was cracked. She had two, large runs in her hose, and she was holding her lipstick like a lollipop when Mrs. Michael Stellar found her.

The Lawnboy noticed what was happening and instructed the ladies to go sit in the living room. He went to the bathroom to help wake up Mrs. Stanley Bigsbee, who had a small gash on her face. He carried her into the living room, put her in a wing back chair and propped pillows all around her. He graciously carried Mrs. Charles Chatterton, who was still on the floor, to a bed.

After all that was taken care of, he started to clean up the mess. The Lawnboy had no sooner cleaned up the dining room table when Bunny Baxley and Beebe Hall jumped up and went out to the kitchen. Bunny Baxley brought out café *brulôt* that Beebe Hall had just lit. She announced that a little coffee would help everyone clear her head.

The party ended rather abruptly. Elizabeth, Mrs. Stanley Bigsbee's daughter, came to get her mother and Mrs.Charles Chatterton. Neither Mr. Stanley Bigsbee nor Mr. Charles Chatteron were in any condition to pick up his wife from the party. They had both passed out at the Bigsbee's residence while waiting for their wives to return. Maribelle Biche left in such a hurry she forgot to ask for the recipes.

[31] *Guy Fawkes was in on the attempted burning of the British Parliament in 1605. The incident known as "The Gunpowder Plot" is still commemorated with bonfires and fireworks every November 5th in various cities in Great Britain. Mr. and Mrs. Elmer Steele have been to several Guy Fawkes celebrations in England, and Beebe Hall's party was a lot like what goes on in her ancestral homeland.*

Beebe Hall and Bunny Baxley poured themselves one last drink before Bunny finally left.

The next morning Beebe Hall remembered the centerpieces she was going to blow up, but she saw that all that was left of them were the red flowers. The fireworks were gone. She had a sneaking suspicion who took them, but her head felt like it was going to explode and that was all she could handle. The recipes were put in the cookbook, but nobody remembered how they tasted.

Flaming Absinthe Cocktail

1 ounce Absinthe
½ ounce Grand Marnier orange liqueur
3 tablespoons of mineral water
1 dash bitters
sugar lump

Shake all the ingredients with ice. Strain into a cocktail glass. Put a sugar lump on a perforated spoon and immerse it in the drink until it is well saturated. Bring the spoon with the sugar lump on it out of the drink and balance it across the glass. Using a match set fire to the sugar lump. Lower the melted sugar lump into the drink.

Beebe insisted on serving this drink even though it was lots of work to make them for all the ladies. The Lawnboy had practiced making them, and even he couldn't keep up. Katrina Canfield had to announce that she was in possession of some rare silver, Absinthe-slotted spoons. Nobody cared. They just wanted to drink. Mrs. Molly McCurdle, who didn't drink much, became interested in this drink when she heard it is sometimes referred to as 'The Green Fairy.'

Flaming *Sambuca*

Pour the *Sambuca* in a glass and light it! Drink it while it is warm.

One usually puts her hand over the glass to douse the flames. Mrs. Charles Chatterton left her hand on her glass too long and burned her hand. It wasn't a bad burn, but it hurt enough so that she had to take several pills to ease the pain. Mrs. Elmer Steele told Maribelle Biche she knew something like this would happen.

Flaming Onion Soup

4 tablespoons unsalted butter
2 large white onions, thinly sliced
1 large yellow onion, thinly sliced
1 large red onion, thinly sliced
1 teaspoon salt
1 teaspoon pepper
3 cups of chicken broth
3 cups of beef broth
3 cups water

7 slices of French bread
2 cups Gruyère cheese, grated

1 cup whiskey
2 tablespoons unsalted butter

In saucepan, melt the butter. Add the onions and cook until the onions are tender. Add salt, pepper, chicken broth, beef broth and water. Bring to a boil and simmer for 1 ½ hours.

Dip slices of French bread into melted butter and toast them in an oven. Sprinkle the Gruyère cheese on top of the bread and broil until the cheese is melted. Heat the whiskey and pour over the onion soup. Pour the soup into individual bowls and top with the French bread.

Mrs. E. O. Bittleduke was getting a little weary of all the fires. She didn't say anything because she knew it was Beebe Hall's passion. The soup was only for show. Other than Mrs. Elmer Steele, nobody touched it.

Flaming Spinach Salad

2 pounds spinach leaves, rinsed, dried and chilled
¾ pound bacon, diced in small pieces
½ cup red wine vinegar
2 teaspoons Worcestershire sauce
1 lemon, juiced
½ cup sugar
½ cup cognac

Sauté bacon. Add the red wine vinegar, Worcestershire sauce, lemon juice and sugar. Stir well. Add the cognac and pour over the spinach leaves. Quickly ignite.

By the time the salad reached the table, Katrina Canfield was getting tired of all the fires, and she jokingly remarked, "Why, you'd think it was the 4th of July around here." Bunny Baxley glared at her, stared her down, and jokingly replied, "You need to lighten up. Get it?"

Brussel Sprouts

1 pound Brussel sprouts
2 tablespoons butter
1 teaspoon salt
1 teaspoon lemon pepper

Wash the Brussel sprouts and drop them in boiling water for 15 minutes. Drain and season with butter, salt and lemon pepper.

Upon seeing the Brussel sprouts, Mrs. Stanley Bigsbee whispered to Mrs. Charles Chatterton, "I think I am going to get sick."

Volcanic Sweet Potatoes

2 large cans of sweet potatoes
4 tablespoons butter, melted
2 cups crackers, crushed
½ bag of large marshmallows

Mash the sweet potatoes and add the melted butter. Mix well and add the crackers. In a shallow, oven-proof pan, mound the sweet potato mixture to resemble a volcano. Cover the tops of the sweet potatoes with marshmallows. Bake at 425°, or until the marshmallows begin to flow out of the top of the potatoes and down the side.

Bunny Baxley played with her sweet potatoes. She said, "When I was a little girl I liked to make a pond in the center of my mashed potatoes, you know with gravy." Mrs. Biche whispered to Mrs. Steele, "Tell her to grow up!"

Steak *Flambé*

6 pounds of flank steak
6 teaspoons cracked peppercorns
1 cup unsalted butter
2 teaspoons Worcestershire sauce
½ teaspoon salt
1 cup brandy
1 cup of cream

Rub the flank steak with the peppercorns, making sure they are lodged in the meat. In a skillet, melt the butter and add the meat. Sauté the meat on both sides. Remove the steak from the skillet and sprinkle with Worcestershire sauce and salt. Keep the meat warm. In the same skillet add the brandy and ignite to flame. Stir in the cream and heat. Ladle this mixture over the steak and serve at once.

Beebe Hall rarely had time to cook for Jimmy. She was secretly hoping there would be some steak left over for him when he came home. She was right. There was enough left for Jimmy, Bunny Baxley's husband, Johnny, and Bunny Baxley's poodle, Fifi.

Flaming Peaches

8 peaches
½ cup butter
½ cup brown sugar
2 teaspoons rum flavoring
1 cup of dark rum

Peal and slice the peaches. Melt the butter and add the brown sugar; stir until well-blended. Add the peaches and the rum flavoring. Cook until the peaches are softened. Add rum and ignite. Put the peaches in compote cups and add sweet cream.

When Beebe Hall and The Lawnboy served the flaming peaches, she said, "This will help you maintain a 'peaches and cream' complexion." What she said didn't make any sense to The Lawnboy, and he rolled his eyes at her comment.

Café *Brulôt*

6 sticks of cinnamon
1 box of whole cloves
peel of 6 lemons
peel of 6 oranges
12 teaspoons sugar
24 ounces of Cognac
3 quarts of coffee, cooked

Mash the cinnamon sticks, cloves, lemon and orange peels and sugar. Stir in the brandy and ignite. When the flame subsides, add the coffee. Strain into heated cups.

Beebe Hall's flaming flambé finally came to an end. For most, it was an exhausting evening. After everyone left, Beebe Hall continued to 'flame' anything in her sight.

69

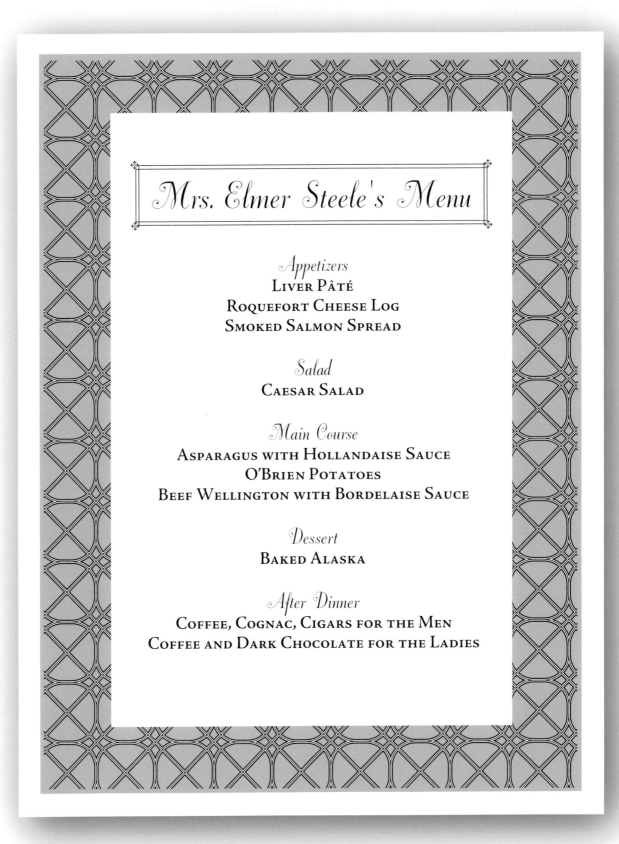

Mrs. Elmer Steele's Menu

Appetizers
LIVER PÂTÉ
ROQUEFORT CHEESE LOG
SMOKED SALMON SPREAD

Salad
CAESAR SALAD

Main Course
ASPARAGUS WITH HOLLANDAISE SAUCE
O'BRIEN POTATOES
BEEF WELLINGTON WITH BORDELAISE SAUCE

Dessert
BAKED ALASKA

After Dinner
COFFEE, COGNAC, CIGARS FOR THE MEN
COFFEE AND DARK CHOCOLATE FOR THE LADIES

MRS. ELMER STEELE'S DINNER PARTY

After Beebe Hall's flambé fiasco, Mrs. Elmer Steele knew without a doubt, that if The Executives' Wives' Cookbook Committees Cookbook was going to become a reality, and not just 'club talk', she would have to reign in the wind and bring back a sense of sanity and structure to the project. She bristled as she said to her husband, Elmer, "If I were president, which I should have been, this quagmire would have never happened. Now I am going to have to turn back the tide, and get this book project sailing out of 'la la' land and in the right direction."

With her competent leadership abilities, and her invaluable knack for directing and organizing, Mrs. Elmer Steele, single-handedly grabbed the helm, adjusted the rudder, raised the sails and changed the course and direction of the cookbook project in mid-stream in order to get The Executives' Wives' Cookbook Committee back on course and above board.

She methodically and brilliantly charted her course before she set sail. She found out when all of the ladies on the cookbook committee would be in town, and quickly sent out lavishly, engraved invitations. She made it clear, that it was imperative that they all be in attendance and with their husbands.

In other words, without being hopelessly rude and in a symbolic way, Mrs. Elmer Steele took out her whistle and blew it to recall them to a workaday world. They all knew she meant business and what she was going to suggest.

Everyone decided they had no choice but to come to the Steele's dinner party, but no one was looking forward to it. The Baxleys, Halls, Chattertons and Bigsbees went to the club for a few 'warm-ups' to enjoy, as Bunny Baxley called it, 'the calm before the storm.' After a few cocktails, Bunny Baxley, who had no trouble speaking her mind, entertained her friends. She jumped on her chair, protruded her stomach, hoisted her glass and sang, "Let's drink to the fat, old bat before we hear her mean-spirited chat." Beebe Hall, imitating Bunny Baxley, jumped up on her chair,

hoisted her glass and chimed in, "With her batons, her bats, or her billy clubs, she'll pound us down to a bunch of stubs." Not to be outdone, Mrs. Stanley Bigsbee, who didn't trust herself on a chair, stood up, hoisted her glass and said, "Oh dear, our poor Sarge Marge, why, oh why is she getting so large?" They all sat down and laughed hysterically, except Mrs. Charles Chatterton. The dear, sweet lady had fallen asleep, but she woke up quickly and said, "Where in the world am I?" Slurring her words, she continued, "I just had a dream. I was in heaven, but then I fell down to hell." Beebe Hall giggled and said, "Hell's bells, of course you're in hell, you're hot to trot." With that they all got up and left.

After the group all arrived at the Steele's home, Mr. Elmer Steele, a large red-headed, fair-skinned Scot, offered them a scotch. Mr. Elmer Steele had hired The Lawnboy to man the bar. He had instructed him to make the drinks stiff, especially the ones he was making for the ladies. Mr. Elmer Steele greeted all the guests as they arrived and immediately engaged in his typical flirtatious mannerisms. He winked at Bunny Baxley when she arrived and said, "My, oh my, aren't you one cute, little, red fox." Bunny Baxley giggled. She was used to him, and Johnny, her husband, knew Mr. Elmer Steele meant no harm. Mrs. Elmer Steele, trying to be lighthearted and act gaily said, "Well, aren't you Miss Spanky Pants." It didn't work. Bunny Baxley glared at Mrs. Elmer Steele so intensely that Mrs. Elmer Steele backed down.

After the encounter, the other guests arrived. Mrs. Christina Pebbleworth-Stafford looked like she was going to a dinner on the Seine, instead of a dinner at the Steele's home. Mrs. Elmer Steele, who did not like Mrs. Christina Pebbleworth-Stafford's attitude or the fact that she put down anything that was English, and extolled everything that was French, decided early on that she was going to put her in her place. She didn't know exactly how, but as luck would have it, a golden opportunity was thrown right in her face.

Mrs. Elmer Steele immediately noticed that Mrs. Christina Pebbleworth-Stafford's hem was hanging down about a quarter of an inch in the back slit of her exquisitely-tailored Chanel skirt. Mrs. Elmer Steele looked at Mrs. Christina Pebbleworth-Stafford and facetiously said, "Oh Christina, it looks like the couture house of Chanel is starting to unravel at the seams. I hope it's not a structural problem." Mrs. Christina Pebbleworth-Stafford turned her head to the back of her skirt to make sure what she was hearing was true. Without saying a word, she angrily left for the bathroom.

Mrs. Elmer Steele directed everyone to the dining room and told them to seat themselves by their name cards. Of course, her seating arrangements were not accidental. With Mr. Elmer Steele at the end of the table, she had purposely put Mrs. Christina Pebbleworth-Stafford to the left of him, and herself to the right of him, so she could keep a close watch on her husband. She knew Mrs. Christina Pebbleworth-Stafford, the 'highbrow of couture mannerisms,' would seek revenge, and she did. Without batting an eyelash, she looked at Mrs. Elmer Steele, and then at Mr. Elmer Steele and said, "Is that your foot I'm feeling?"

Mrs. Elmer Steele noticeably scowled and acted like nothing had taken place. She said, "Ladies, I hope you enjoy the meal I have personally prepared for you without any help. [32] These are the recipes I am submitting for The Executives' Wives' Cookbook. I was concerned that our book had too many French recipes in it and not enough English ones." She looked at Mrs. Christina Pebbleworth-Stafford and whispered, "God save the Queen." Mrs. Christina Pebbleworth-Stafford opened her dark large eyes, glared at Mrs. Elmer Steele and said, "Um, would you get on with the plot?"

Mrs. Elmer Steele, not missing a beat, ignored Christina, and addressed the group again. "Ladies, we have to get serious. We will either sink or swim." Mrs. Charles Chatterton and Mrs. Stanley Bigsbee both perked up. Mrs. Charles Chatterton, who was awake and unusually coherent, tried to lighten things up by saying, "Charlotte and I know, if we swim in synchronized unison, we hold each other up. Isn't that right, Charlotte?" Mrs. Stanley Bigsbee, who had her compact open and was busy freshening up her lipstick didn't really hear what her friend was saying. Nobody else could understand what she meant, but everyone laughed. The party lightened up and everyone was relieved.

After the caloric, laden meal, Mr. Elmer Steele announced that the men should proceed to the library for some more scotch, socialization and cigars. The ladies sat and drank at the table.

After the party was over, The Lawnboy cleaned up and consoled Mrs. Elmer Steele who said she felt like she was coming down with a migraine. The Lawnboy told her that her bull dog door knocker was missing. "What else?," she lamented as she grabbed for the pharmaceuticals. She was glad it was over, secretly glad she wasn't the president of The Executives' Wives' Cookbook Committee and felt like she told her husband, Elmer, as he was snoring and sailing off to sleep, "The whole bloody thing was a travesty." She lay awake, secretly wondering if she had lost her ability to 'control the wind and the waves' and what could she do 'to get back to shore.'

---

[32] *It was obvious that preparing and cooking the dinner did take its toll on Mrs. Elmer Steele. She was dressed like a frumpy Anglo-Saxon sheepherder and looked like she was scoured with a steel brush. She was the color of a beet root, either from the steam in the kitchen or the 'steam' in her mind.*

Liver Pâté

16 ounces liver sausage
16 ounces cream cheese
1 cup onion
2 teaspoons thyme
8 tablespoons butter
6 tablespoons sherry
6 tablespoons whipping cream

Mix the liver sausage, cream cheese, onion and thyme. Add the sherry and whipping cream. Put the pâté in a pretty, small bowl and serve with thin breads or crackers.

Mr. Elmer Steele enjoyed liver pâté, so Mrs. Elmer Steele decided to serve it. She wished she hadn't, the way he was acting.

Roquefort Cheese Log

16 ounces *Roquefort* cheese
8 ounces cream cheese
4 teaspoons dry mustard
2 tablespoons Worcestershire sauce
¼ cup cognac
½ cups pecans
½ cup parsley, chopped

Crumble the *Roquefort* cheese and blend with the cream cheese. Add the dry mustard, Worcestershire sauce and cognac. Stir in pecans. Chill. Shape into logs and cover logs with parsley. Serve with crackers.

Mrs. Charles Chatterton was hoping Mrs. Elmer Steele would have something to nibble on that the ladies would enjoy, but no such luck.

Smoked Salmon Spread

16 ounces cream cheese
½ cup cream
1 green onion, chopped
1 teaspoon lemon juice
1 dash hot sauce
1 cup smoked salmon, shredded

Mix the cream cheese and cream. Stir in the chopped onion, lemon juice and smoked salmon. Serve with crackers or small breads.

Bunny Baxley took some smoked salmon, put it in a napkin and fed it to the Steele's house cat. The cat ate it quickly and then threw up all over the oriental rug in the living room. Mrs. Elmer Steele was in a huff when she realized what happened. Everyone, including Bunny Baxley, acted surprised when Mrs. Elmer Steele asked the ladies if they knew who fed the cat.

Caesar Salad

2 heads Romaine lettuce

Dressing
1 ½ cups olive oil
6 tablespoons lemon juice
4 tablespoons onions, minced
1 garlic clove, crushed
1 teaspoon dry mustard
1 teaspoon salt
1 teaspoon pepper

Croutons
4 slices bread
½ cup olive oil
½ teaspoon garlic salt

Topping
2 eggs
1 cup Parmesan cheese, grated
anchovy fillets

Cube 4 slices of bread. Sauté the bread in olive oil and garlic salt until browned. Take the croutons out of the pan and drain on paper towel.

Pour the olive oil, lemon juice, onions, garlic, dry mustard, salt and pepper in a jar and shake. Refrigerate overnight. Tear up 2 heads of Romaine lettuce. Mix in the dressing and toss. Toss in the croutons. Slightly whisk the egg; put it over the lettuce and toss again. Add Parmesan cheese and anchovy fillets before serving.

Mrs. Charles Chatterton tried to eat the salad, but gagged on the raw egg. She went to the bathroom, and like the Steele's cat, threw up.

Asparagus with Hollandaise Sauce

18 asparagus stalks
2 teaspoons salt
1 teaspoon pepper

Clean asparagus and wash thoroughly. Tie 6 stalks together and stand them upright in boiling water. Cook 18-20 minutes or until soft, but not mushy.

Hollandaise sauce
1 cup butter
4 egg yolks, slightly beaten
1 teaspoon salt
1 teaspoon white pepper
½ teaspoon cayenne pepper
4 tablespoons lemon juice
½ cup parsley, minced

Cream the butter and put ½ cup in double boiler with the egg yolks, salt, white pepper, cayenne pepper and lemon juice. On very low heat, cook until the mixture begins to thicken. After it starts to thicken, add another ½ cup of butter. Stirring constantly, cook for approximately 20 minutes. Mix in minced parsley. Serve the Hollandaise sauce hot.

Mrs. Michael Stellar told Mrs. E.O. Bittleduke that she thought the asparagus was woody. That's the first time anyone has heard her complain.

O'Brien Potatoes

10 potatoes

2 onions, chopped
1 green pepper, chopped
½ cup pimiento
¾ cup olive oil

1 teaspoon salt
½ teaspoon pepper
¼ teaspoon paprika

Boil potatoes, drain and peel. Dice potatoes and set aside in bowl. In a large skillet cook onions and green pepper in olive oil until tender. Add the potatoes, salt, pepper and paprika. Cook for approximately 15 minutes, or until the potatoes are browned.

Mrs. Christina Pebbleworth-Stafford didn't think much of the O'Brien. She said to Maribelle Biche, "I think that's something they serve on farms, not at a dinner party in the city."

Beef Wellington with *Bordelaise* Sauce

3 pounds beef tenderloin
2 teaspoons pepper
1 tablespoon melted butter

In a roasting pan place beef tenderloin that has been peppered. Brush the beef with the melted butter and roast for 40-50 minutes at 425°. Remove from oven.

Onion/mushroom sauce
½ cup butter, plus 2 tablespoons
1 onion, chopped
1 pound mushrooms, sliced
1 teaspoon thyme
1 teaspoon salt
1 teaspoon pepper

3 egg whites

2 egg yolks
½ cup cream

In a sauce pan, cook the onions until they are translucent. Add the mushrooms, 2 tablespoons butter, thyme, salt and pepper. Cook until the mushrooms are dark and dehydrated.

Liver pâté
16 ounces liver sausage
16 ounces cream cheese
1 cup onion
2 teaspoons thyme
8 tablespoons butter
6 tablespoons sherry
6 tablespoons whipping cream

Mix the liver sausage, cream cheese, onion, thyme and butter. Add the sherry and whipping cream.

Puff pastry dough (purchased)
Roll out the puff pastry dough to a size that will engulf the beef tenderloin, and place on a large cookie sheet. Spread liver pâté over the dough, and then top with the onion/mushroom mixture. Place beef atop mixture. Bring sides of dough up and crimp together. Brush it with the egg whites. Slightly cream the egg yolks and cream. Brush egg yolk/cream mixture over dough. Bake for approximately 30 to 35 minutes at 375°.

Bordelaise Sauce

4 tablespoons butter
2 shallots, finely chopped
1 garlic clove, finely chopped
1 small onion, chopped
3 carrots, sliced
1 bay leaf
2 parsley sprigs

4 tablespoons flour
2 cans beef bouillon

1 cup red wine
½ teaspoon salt
½ teaspoon black pepper

In saucepan, melt butter and add shallots, garlic, onion, carrots, bay leaf and parsley sprigs. Sauté until the onion is transparent. Remove from heat and add the flour. Stir in 2 cans of beef bouillon, and simmer for 15 minutes. Add red wine, salt and pepper.

All the men complimented Mrs. Elmer Steele on her Beef Wellington. She puffed up with pride, and soaked in the adulations, which, as of late had been few and far between.

Baked Alaska

Sponge cake
4 eggs
1 cup sugar
2 tablespoons lemon juice
¼ teaspoon salt
⅛ teaspoon lemon flavoring

Beat the egg yolks until they are lemon-colored. Gradually add the sugar and continue to beat. Add the lemon juice, salt and lemon flavoring.

In a separate bowl, beat the egg whites until they form peaks. Alternating the egg whites and flour, fold them into the egg yolk mixture.

Pour the batter into two spring form pan. Bake for approximately 50 minutes in a 350° oven. Cool.

Meringue
6 egg whites
½ teaspoon cream of tartar
1 cup sugar

Beat the egg whites with the cream of tartar until they are stiff. Gradually beat in 1 cup of sugar and continue to beat until the meringue is glossy.

Place a circular piece of brown paper on a cookie sheet. Center the sponge cake on it. Pile two quarts of hard strawberry ice cream on top of the cake. Cover the cake and ice cream with a thick coating of meringue. Bake at 500° for 4-5 minutes.

The Baked Alaska was lovely and delicious. There was a lot left over, and everyone knew that Mrs. Elmer Steele would be indulging in the spoils, even if most other people would have discarded the soggy mess.

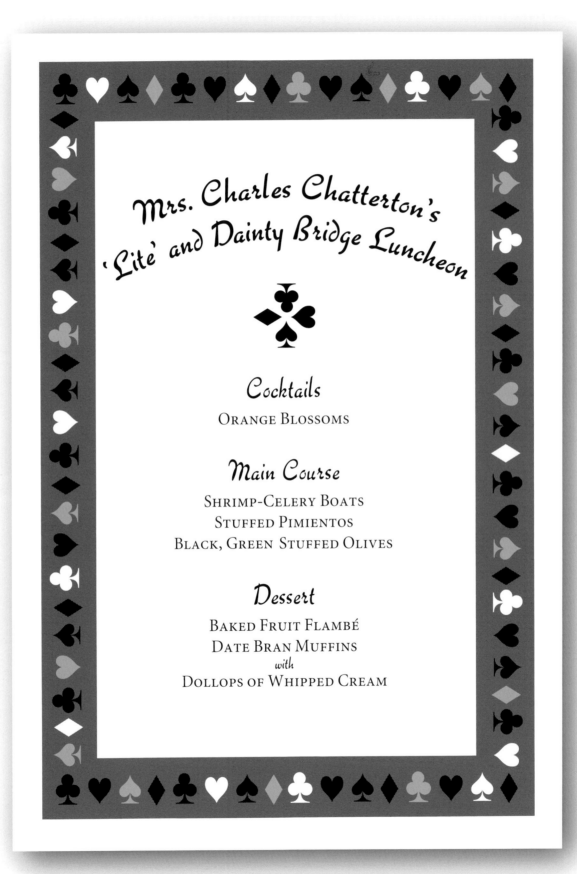

Mrs. Charles Chatterton's 'Lite' and Dainty Bridge Luncheon

Cocktails

ORANGE BLOSSOMS

Main Course

SHRIMP-CELERY BOATS
STUFFED PIMIENTOS
BLACK, GREEN STUFFED OLIVES

Dessert

BAKED FRUIT FLAMBÉ
DATE BRAN MUFFINS
with
DOLLOPS OF WHIPPED CREAM

MRS. CHARLES CHATTERTON'S 'LITE' BRIDGE AND BIRTHDAY LUNCHEON

Mrs. Charles Chatterton decided to host a bridge luncheon to try out her recipes for The Executives' Wives' Cookbook on Beebe Hall's birthday. Mrs. Charles Chatterton was several years older than Beebe Hall, but she had always admired Beebe Hall's spunk, and her ability to light up a room! She once told Beebe Hall, "I was just like you twenty years ago. Now it takes me all day to get ready, and then I fall asleep before I get any place." Beebe Hall has always idolized Mrs. Charles Chatterton. She loved her clothes, make-up and the fact that she, at her age, is still shapely. Besides, they have a few things in common; they both smoke Old Golds, they both drive red cars,[33] and they have both loved Slow Gin Fizzes since their teen-age years.

Mrs. Charles Chatterton liked to serve a 'lite' bridge luncheon. Since everyone has always talked about watching their weight, or pretending that they were,[34] she has always served a 'guilt-free' luncheon.

The ladies of The Executives' Wives' Cookbook Committee always enjoy going to Charlotte's home. This fun-loving, elegant lady goes out of her way to make everyone feel comfortable. She always has had ashtrays placed so as to indicate that smoking is permissible; and she always has lots of vodka, lots of gin, lots of ice, lots of lemons, and lots of other essentials on hand.

It is rare when someone can't make it to a bridge luncheon day at the Chatterton's home. Everyone on The Executives' Wives' Cookbook Committee loves to play bridge. The problem is that Mrs. Elmer Steele, Maribelle Biche, Mrs. Christina Pebbleworth-Stafford and Katrina Canfield are notoriously and fiercely competitive, and play to win. They are not afraid to go for the jugular when they deem it necessary.[35]

Ladies like Beebe Hall, Bunny Baxley, and Mrs. Stanley Bigsbee come for the drinks and the fun, and don't let anyone get in their way. Mrs. Molly McCurdle, Mrs. Samuel Squire, Martha Payne and Doris Dupré are visibly anxious; and the rest, Mrs. Grant Goldman-Hues, Mrs. Jonathan Hurlinger, Mrs. Michael Stellar, and Mrs. E.O. Bittleduke take everything in stride, and believe that 'bridge,' after all, is only a game.

---

[33] Mrs. Charles Chatterton drives a red Cadillac convertible, and Beebe Hall drives a little hot, fire-engine red Alfa Romeo sports car.

[34] Everyone had noticed that Mrs. Elmer Steele had put on a few pounds over the winter, especially 'in the middle'. They didn't know if it was from food that she was eating, or something that was 'eating her'. Nobody said anything, but as Mrs. Charles Chatterton, confidentially said to Beebe, "The poor dear, if she doesn't watch out, she's going to look just like her Baked Alaska, and it's going to take more than her Beef Wellington to keep Elmer at home. He's out and about enough as it is already."

[35] Mrs. Elmer Steele and Maribelle Biche verbally reprimand their partners when they feel they have messed up. Mrs. Christina Pebbleworth-Stafford and Katrina Canfield are more subtle. They are masters of intimidation, i.e. 'if looks could kill'. These four ladies always try to get the bid.

A day of bridge takes its toll on Mrs. Charles Chatterton, and sometimes it's hard for her to last the whole day. Once she disappeared, only to be found sleeping on her bed, wrapped in her mink. Poor dear, no one has ever questioned her intentions.

This particular luncheon was no different than the others, except that Mrs. Charles Chatterton had prepared a fruit *flambé* in honor of Beebe Hall's birthday. Beebe Hall got to light it; Bunny Baxley left the fruit but drank the juice; and everyone else took at least two bites of it and thought Mrs. Charles Chatterton had gone way above the call of duty to make it such a special day. After everyone left, and Mrs. Charles Chatterton wanted to relax with an Old Gold, she summoned The Lawnboy and said, "Have you seen my table lighter?" He said he hadn't seen it, but he'd keep his eye out for it.

Orange Blossoms

3 ounces gin
1 ounce orange juice, freshly squeezed
1 dash lime juice
½ teaspoon powdered sugar

Mix the gin, orange juice, lime juice and powdered sugar. Vigorously shake the ingredients with ice. Strain into a cocktail glass and garnish with an orange wedge.

This recipe is Mrs. Charles Chatterton's personal concoction. She added 1 more ounce of gin, and 1 less ounce of orange juice than what is in a standard Orange Blossom cocktail. As she once told The Executives' Wives' Cookbook Committee at one of her bridge luncheons, "The only thing I water down is my lawn."

Shrimp & Celery Boats

16 6 inch firm celery stalks
6 pounds of shrimp, cooked, chilled and finely chopped
1 ⅛ cups butter
1 ½ teaspoons salt
1 teaspoon pepper
1 teaspoon cayenne pepper
1 bunch of parsley, finely chopped

Put the shrimp in a bowl. Combine butter, salt, pepper, and cayenne pepper and thoroughly mix it with the shrimp. Chill. Stuff into celery stalks and garnish with chopped parsley. Arrange the celery boats on a fancy tray.

When Mrs. Jonathan Hurlinger took a bite of her shrimp and celery boat, she started to choke on the celery string that got stuck in her throat. Everyone saw it, but she recovered quickly. Bunny Baxley rushed over with an Orange Blossom cocktail and told her to drink it fast to clear her throat. Needless to say, she didn't eat any more of it. Something like this has never happened to her before.

Red Stuffed Pimientos

2 jars large pimientos

2 cups of small shrimp, cooked and chilled
2 tablespoons onion, minced finely
2 tablespoons celery, chopped finely
1 cup of cream cheese, softened

2 tablespoons parsley, finely chopped

Combine the shrimp, onion and celery. Fold in the cream cheese. Fill the pimientos with the cream cheese mixture. Chill.

Mrs. Charles Chatterton likes anything red, from Cadillacs to lipstick, to slow gin fizzes, to pimientos. She thought this recipe would add a little 'Latin flavor' to her luncheon, even though nobody raved about it. Maribelle Biche didn't even ask for the recipe.

Black & Green Stuffed Olives

Mrs. Charles Chatterton didn't enjoy cooking as much as she did entertaining. Whenever she entertained she always served both black and green stuffed olives. It was for nostalgic reasons. The night Charles popped the question, he took an olive out of his dirty martini and popped it in his mouth. It was at the Fontainebleau in Miami Beach, and she will never forget it. Besides, she knows that olives are good filler foods.

Baked Fruit *Flambé*
for Beebe's Birthday

1 cup water
1 cup brown sugar
½ cup lemon juice
½ cup orange juice
8 teaspoons lemon peel, grated
8 tablespoons orange peel, grated

In saucepan, combine the water, brown sugar, lemon and orange juice, and lemon and orange peel. Simmer on low heat. Cool slightly.

6 cups of brown sugar
5 teaspoons cinnamon
½ teaspoon ground cloves

In a bowl, combine brown sugar with cinnamon and cloves.

8 fresh peaches, skinned and halved
8 firm, pears, skinned and halved
1 large can of pineapple chunks, drained
4 oranges, peeled and sectioned

4 cups of rum

Dip the fruit in the first mixture, and then dip it in the second mixture. Arrange the coated fruit in a stylish serving/baking dish, and bake at 350° for 20 minutes. Take it out of the oven and pour rum that has been heated and ignite over the fruit.

The recipe called for two cups of rum but Mrs. Charles Chatterton doubled it to four cups, just for Beebe Hall. She let Beebe Hall have the honor of igniting the rum and pouring it over the fruit. For Beebe Hall it was better than having a birthday cake.

Date Bran Muffins
with Dollops of Whipped Cream

2 cups all-purpose flour, sifted
3 teaspoons baking powder
½ teaspoon salt
¼ cup brown sugar
½ cups dates, chopped
1 cup bran
1 cup whole milk
1 egg
¼ cup vegetable oil

In a mixing bowl, sift the flour, baking powder, salt and sugar together. Stir in the chopped dates. In another bowl, mix the bran with the milk, and let it soak for 10 minutes. Add the egg and vegetable oil to the bran and milk mixture. Beat well. Pour this mixture into the flour/baking/powder/salt/sugar mixture. Stir only until the dry ingredients are moistened. Spoon the batter into muffin tins that have been filled with cupcake wrappers. Fill each tin only two-thirds full. Bake at 400° for about 25 minutes, or until browned. Cool. When serving, add a dollop of whipped cream on the top of each muffin.

Even though Mrs. Charles Chatterton had sixteen for lunch, she only made twelve muffins. She knew most of the ladies wouldn't take one, but she made them in honor of Beebe's birthday. She thought they resembled cupcakes. Mrs. E.O. Bittleduke watched to see who would take one. She had looked in Dr. Bittleduke's confidential files and she knew exactly which ladies needed to eat one to remain regular.

Mrs. Stanley Bigsbee's
LaLaLaLa Lipstick
Luncheon

COCKTAILS
Marilyn Monroes
Pink Clouds
Pink Ladies

APPETIZERS
Red Cheese Ball
Pickled Beets
Boiled Radishes

SALADS
Shrimp Salad
Salmon Mousse
Assorted Imported Crackers

DESSERTS
Raspberry Mousse
Legendary, Luscious, Lavish, Lipstick Lovelies

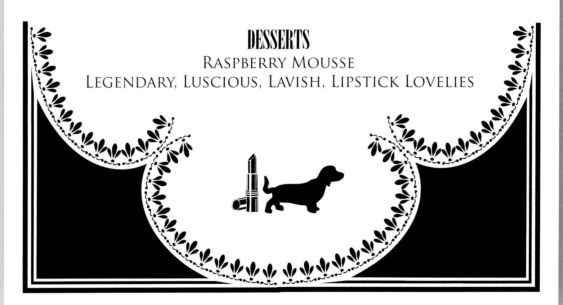

MRS. STANLEY BIGSBEE'S KICK-OFF LUNCHEON FOR THE LA LA LA LA LIPSTICK BALL

Because of her conditions, entertaining was becoming more difficult for the lovely and lively Mrs. Stanley Bigsbee. She decided, as she told Bunny her co-chair of the La La La La Lipstick Ball, to 'paint two lips with one brush', and hold the kick-off Lipstick Ball luncheon in conjunction with the luncheon, showcasing her recipes for The Executives' Wives' Cookbook Committee.

Bunny Baxley was sympathetic and well aware of Mrs. Stanley Bigsbee's conditions and dilemma. "Not to worry," she reassured Mrs. Stanley Bigsbee. "Remember, I'm the muscle girl behind this event and I promise I will help you put it together so everything will be as perfect as a well-made martini."

Two days before the big event was to take place at the Bigsbee's residence, Bunny Baxley went over to help Mrs. Stanley Bigsbee finish up the details for the luncheon, and sample the special drinks she had chosen to serve with the food. Bunny Baxley was relieved that Mrs. Stanley Bigsbee had already taken care of the big stuff,[36] and they just had the fun stuff left to do.

Mrs. Stanley Bigsbee or, rather her daughter, Elizabeth, as it had turned out, had instructed the caterer on the food, and how her mother wanted it served. She told them, "My mother wants to make sure that drinks are replenished immediately. The food should be well-garnished, but if you run out, it's not a big deal. Most of the ladies are on diets anyway."

Elizabeth contracted The Lawnboy, who was getting to be Mrs. Stanley Bigsbee's second 'right hand', to mow the day of the event. He reassured her he would stay to help with the party, clean-up, and other unexpected things that might pop up. "He's such a trooper," Mrs. Stanley Bigsbee told Bunny Baxley. Bunny Baxley replied, "What would we do without him? I guess we have to call him, not me, the muscle girl behind the event."

Bunny Baxley was like a kid in a candy store when she saw all the lavish favors Mrs. Stanley Bigsbee had purchased for the luncheon. There were tubes of MAX Factor lipstick in all the latest colors and beautiful gold compacts with matching pill boxes. "Look at these beautiful shades of lipsticks in all the wonderful shades of merlots and roses," Bunny said excitedly as she opened all the tubes of lipstick, and played with them like they were mechanical toys.

[36] Mrs. Stanley Bigsbee's daughter, Elizabeth, was the one that had handled the 'big stuff' for her mother.

Mrs. Stanley Bigsbee had gone all out for this luncheon. She had engaged a MAX Factor rep. from her favorite department store to come and give a demonstration on 'the latest etiquette on the art of applying lipstick' at the table after the main course. Even though her best friend, Mrs. Charles Chatterton, bless her heart, had offered to give a demonstration on lipstick etiquette, Mrs. Stanley Bigsbee, knowing her conditions, decided to leave nothing to chance. Actually, it was her daughter, Elizabeth, who strongly encouraged her mother to hire the rep. Even the food and beverages on the menu were designed to color-coordinate with lipstick colors.

The day of the luncheon Bunny Baxley, as promised, came early to make sure everything was in order, and to help Mrs. Stanley Bigsbee relax over a couple of cocktails. As expected, Mrs. Charles Chatterton arrived early to join them in cocktails.

Mrs. Stanley Bigsbee was honored that all the ladies of The Executives' Wives' Cookbook Committee made a concerted effort to be at her luncheon. No one was missing, not even Martha Payne. Bunny Baxley helped serve the cocktails, and after everyone was in 'fun form', the ladies were seated for their luncheon and demonstration on applying lipstick. The MAX Factor rep. looked at the ladies around the table, thought to herself, 'Oh dear, what have I gotten myself into?', and said, "I will first do the demonstration, and then we will practice the art, after you have eaten the main course." The rep. began, "Ladies, the first thing I want you to do is indiscreetly open your compacts, and get comfortable with them." As instructed, and in unison, the ladies opened their compacts,[37] except for Mrs. Charles Chatterton who was having trouble with her latch. The rep. went over to help Mrs. Charles Chatterton, whose fingers were shaking, open her compact. Bunny saw what was happening, and hurriedly got her another cocktail.

The next item on the rep's. agenda was to help each lady pick a shade of lipstick that would be the most flattering. As the rep. soon found out, old habits don't die fast, and each lady knew exactly what shade of lipstick she wanted to use. Mrs. Grant-Goldman Hues went for the lavender shade, Mrs. Charles Chatterton and Mrs. Stanley Bigsbee opted for the most saturated red color that was available. Doris Dupré wanted the darkest shade of lipstick, and Beebe Hall wanted one that was closest to the color of a fire engine. Bunny chose the red/orange color that was closest to the color of her hair. As expected, Mrs. Michael Stellar wanted a rich looking creamy pink color, and Mrs. Molly McCurdle went for the cotton candy-colored lipstick.

Both Katrina Canfield and Mrs. Christina Pebbleworth-Stafford chose the same color. After this happened, Mrs. Christina Pebbleworth-Stafford, boldly and with her attitude showing, announced to the ladies that the lipstick of choice for her was made by Chanel. She didn't do it to make Mrs. Stanley Bigsbee feel bad, but she deemed it necessary to say because it was one way she could make a statement to Katrina Canfield who was beginning to be her constant competitor and an irritant to her. Each of the other ladies chose various shades of red colors that they believed were the right shades for their lips.

After the main course and another cocktail, the demonstration on applying lipstick started. The rep. decided to demonstrate on Mrs. Charles Chatterton because, after watching her struggle to get her compact open, and looking at the way she had applied her morning lipstick, she knew Mrs. Charles Chatterton might have a little trouble, and as it turned out, it was the rep. that ran into big trouble.

The rep. instructed Mrs. Charles Chatterton to put her head back so she could apply the lipstick, and she eagerly cooperated. She rather enjoyed the attention that was thrust upon her. The rep. began by applying a lipstick remover to get Mrs. Charles Chatterton's morning lipstick off. As she soon found out, even MAX Factor's remover didn't touch the color that was obviously, permanently and indelibly colored on her lips. However, she ignored the problem, and continued her demonstration. Just as she was starting to put the lipstick on Mrs. Charles Chatterton's upper lip, her

[37] *To anyone within listening range, the sound of the 'click of the compacts' was akin to the sound that one heard when in 1959 the infamous bullfighter Antonio Ordenez clicked his heels in front of Ernest Hemingway, his brother-in-law, and other famous people before he held out the red cape to engage the bull at the bullfighting ring in Rondo Spain*

head bobbed forward and down. The lipstick in the rep's. hand followed the course of the bobbed head, and she inadvertently drew a lipstick line on Mrs. Charles Chatteron's face from her upper lip all the way up to and into her eyeball. When the lipstick hit her eyeball, she woke up, bobbed her head backwards and the rep., lipstick still in hand, automatically drew a line from her eye down to her lip. Mrs. Charles Chatterton, not sure what had just happened, slurred something about liking the color and taste of Slow Gin Fizzes. The rep., visibly shaken, hurriedly got out her MAX Factor remover and cleaned the lipstick lines that were drawn up and down on Mrs. Charles Chatterton's face. [38] As best as she could, she finished putting lipstick on Mrs. Charles Chatterton's lips.

Nobody commented on what had just happened, but everyone told Mrs. Charles Chatterton how beautiful she looked. Immediately both Bunny Baxley and Mrs. Stanley Bigsbee went to get Mrs. Charles Chatteron another drink. As everyone knew, Mrs. Samuel Squire and Martha Payne both left to go the bathroom to take a pill. Everyone else asked for another cocktail, and The Lawnboy was kept busy mixing and serving drinks.

Right before dessert, the rep. told the others to practice, and that she was sorry she had to leave immediately for another demonstration. The ladies didn't care. They thought she was boring anyway. Besides, they all felt confident that they knew how to put their lipstick on in proper and appropriate ways.

After dessert and a few more drinks, Mrs. Stanley Bigsbee and Bunny Baxley handed out the La La La La Lipstick Ball committee assignments to each of the ladies. She thanked the ladies for coming and told them she had the pill boxes personally monogrammed for each of them. As the ladies were busy opening their purses and transferring their pills to their new pill boxes, Doris Dupré, in her 'five-finger discount' way, pocketed the surplus lipstick favors.
The caterer and The Lawnboy cleared the table and washed the dishes. It was not an easy job, because every cocktail glass was imprinted with lipstick, as was every white linen napkin. The Lawnboy had to use mineral spirits to remove the lipstick imprints on the cocktail glasses. The napkins had to be discarded.

Marilyn Monroe Cocktail

4 ounces champagne
2 ounce apple brandy
1 teaspoon grenadine syrup
4 Maraschino cherries

Pour all ingredients into a champagne saucer and stir. Serve with two cherries on two sticks in very fancy glasses.

Mrs. Stanley Bigsbee received this recipe from Bunny Baxley who told her it is a good 'start-up' drink.

Pink Cloud

4 ounces vodka
4 ounces white rum
2 ounces grenadine
8 ounces pineapple juice
4 cups cracked ice

Put above ingredients in a blender, and blend to a consistency of a Piña Colada.

These were a hit! The Lawnboy had to make four more batches of them!

Pink Ladies

1 jigger gin
1 tablespoon lemon juice
1 tablespoon grenadine syrup
1 egg white
1 teaspoon cream
½ cup cracked ice

Shake ingredients with ice and strain into a cocktail glass.

These were the favorite of Mrs. Molly McCurdle because she liked the name of the drink.

[38] *The lines on her face resembled a road map of the Napa Valley following Highway 29 from the American Canyon to Calistoga and back down again.*

Red Cheese Ball

½ pound Cheddar cheese, finely grated
4 ounces of cream cheese, softened
4 tablespoons sherry
½ teaspoon Worcestershire sauce
⅛ teaspoon onion salt
⅛ teaspoon garlic salt
⅛ teaspoon celery salt
1 cup red bell pepper, finely chopped

With a mixer, mix the Cheddar cheese and cream cheese. Add the sherry, Worcestershire's sauce, onion salt, garlic salt, and celery salt. Shape the mixture into a large ball, wrap in foil and refrigerate. Before serving roll the cheese ball into the finely-chopped, red pepper.

Beebe Hall thought the red cheese ball looked like a cherry bomb. She was trying to figure out how she could make one and ignite it.

Pickled Beets

2 bunches of fresh garden beets
½ cup vinegar
¾ teaspoon salt
6 whole cloves

Boil the beets until soft. Remove the beets and add the vinegar, salt and whole cloves to the beet juice and bring to a boil. Pour this mixture over the beets and chill for at least 8 hours before serving. Make a presentation when serving!

These are Mrs. Charles Chatterton's favorites. After she ate, you couldn't tell if she had lipstick or beet stains on her teeth. The poor dear. Her illness has started to manifest itself in many ways. Her dear friend, Mrs. Stanley Bigsbee, handed her a tissue to clean off her teeth, but she sneezed into it and threw it away.

Boiled Radishes

3 bunches of large radishes

Cut large radishes in half and boil for 15 minutes. Spear the radishes with a colored toothpick and serve.

Martha Payne got the hiccups from the radishes, and became so flustered she immediately left the party.

Shrimp Salad

1 ½ pounds of shrimp, cooked and deveined
2 cups mayonnaise
4 teaspoons prepared mustard
2 teaspoons lemon juice
2 teaspoons salt
¼ teaspoon pepper
2 tablespoons parsley, chopped
4 cups celery, thinly sliced
2 tablespoons onion, finely chopped

head of iceberg lettuce
paprika

Cook shrimp and chill. Combine mayonnaise, mustard, lemon juice, salt and pepper. Add parsley, celery and onions. Add shrimp. Cover and refrigerate until ready to serve. Serve on individual salad plates on which a bed of shredded lettuce has been placed. Sprinkle with paprika.

This is an old 'stand-by' recipe that everyone has made, but nobody really likes to eat.

Salmon Mousse

1 envelope plain gelatin
½ cup boiling water
¼ cup cold water
3 small cans salmon, boneless
¾ cup mayonnaise
½ cup celery, finely diced
½ cup cucumber, peeled and finely diced
½ teaspoon salt
⅛ teaspoon white pepper
2 tablespoons fresh parsley, chopped
1 cup strawberries
pimiento pieces

Dissolve gelatin in boiling water; then add cold water. Set aside. Open the cans of salmon and check to make sure there are no bones or dark skin. Discard any parts that are not desirable. Mix the mayonnaise with dissolved gelatin. Combine celery, cucumber, salt, pepper and parsley in a large bowl and mix with the mayonnaise/gelatin mixture. Place the mousse ingredients into a large, buttered fish-shaped mold.

Right before serving, unmold onto a bed of shredded lettuce that has been mixed with sliced strawberries. Decorate eyes and mouth of 'fish' with pieces of red pimiento.

Bunny Baxley said, "I can't eat it because it looks like a real fish, and I'm a vegetarian so I don't eat meat." Mrs. Christina Pebbleworth-Stafford rolled her eyes at Maribelle Biche, and whispered, "How dumb can one get?"

Raspberry Mousse

2 pints of raspberries
3 egg whites
¼ cup sugar
1 cup whipping cream
½ cup sugar
1 teaspoon vanilla extract

Clean and wash berries. Crush the berries, and add the sugar and egg whites. Beat them until they are fluffy.

Whip cream, slowly adding sugar and vanilla extract. Carefully fold the two mixtures together and spoon mousse into a large, glass bowl or individual parfait glasses. Decorate with dollops of whipped cream and whole raspberries.

In her haughty way, Katrina Canfield said, "How cute; this whole menu is red." Bunny Baxley stared her down , and to everyone's amazement Katrina Canfield appeared to feel uncomfortable.

Legendary, Luscious, Lavish, Lipstick Lovelies

1 ½ cups butter
1 ¼ cups white sugar
2 small eggs
2 teaspoons vanilla extract

3 cups flour
1 ½ teaspoons baking soda
1 teaspoon baking powder

Frosting
1 bag marshmallows
red food coloring

Cream the butter and sugar until smooth. Beat in the eggs and the vanilla extract. Combine the flour, baking soda and baking powder in a separate bowl. Gradually blend the two mixtures. Roll the dough into the shape of lips and place on a cookie sheet. Bake at 375° oven for 8 to 9 minutes. When cool, remove from rack and frost with marshmallows that have been melted in a saucepan. Add a few drops of red food coloring to the marshmallow mix.

These were a hit! Mrs. Charles Chatterton wanted to save her cookie and bring it to the MAX Factor counter at her favorite department store to see if they could match up the red on the cookie with a tube of lipstick.

Mrs. Molly McCurdle's Gazebo Luncheon

Cocktails & Beverages
Strawberry Juleps with Mint
Lemon-Mint Tea

Soup
Chilled Cucumber with Rose Petals

Salad
Wilted Dandelion
with Nasturtium & Violet Flowers

Bread
Lemon Loaf

Main Course
Asparagus Soufflé

Dessert
Summer Fruit Cake
Petticoat Tails

Treats & Yummies
Lollipops
Shirley Temples

MRS. MOLLY MCCURDLE'S GAZEBO LUNCHEON PARTY

Mrs. Molly McCurdle was thankful that her husband, Kent McCurdle, encouraged her to become involved with The Executives' Wives' Cookbook Committee. She was thrilled that she was put on a committee that was interested in helping both puppies and children in distress.

So, it is no wonder, that when she was hosting The Executives' Wives' Cookbook Committee she wanted everything to be as pretty and pink and perfect as possible. She decided her large and beautiful enchanted white gazebo on the point was the perfect setting to premier the recipes she had chosen to debut for The Executives' Wives' Cookbook Committee.

Mrs. Molly McCurdle enlisted the help of countless people to make sure her party was perfect. The Lawnboy became her right-hand man. He spent the whole week before the party with her, carefully listening to her go over serving protocol, serving details, clean-up protocol, clean-up details, and of course, the lawn details. She trusted him. She was grateful he always did exactly what she told him to do, and looked good while he was doing it.

She hired her trusted caterer, the same one she had used for her twin daughters' christening party several years ago. She even found out the name of a Southern Baptist prayer group that prayed for good weather for people who were hosting outside parties and weddings. She called them, enlisted their services, and sent them a generous check for their prayers. It worked.

On the day of the gazebo party, the weather couldn't have been better. With the blue skies, yellow sun, wispy white clouds, low humidity and warm weather, all was grand and glorious. The only thing in the air was a soft gentle breeze that was carrying bees and butterflies who were flitting around all her beautiful flowers that were dressed in full summer bloom.

Mrs. Molly McCurdle, dressed in her pretty pinks from head to toe, was in her gazebo when her guests arrived. She had instructed her valets to park cars and to escort the ladies to the gazebo. Mrs. Stanley

Bigsbee and Mrs. Charles Chatterton arrived together, and the valets decided that they needed three of them to help these two ladies who were a little wobbly on their feet. Maribelle Biche and Mrs. Elmer Steele refused help and let the valets know they could and would make it to the gazebo on their own. Bunny Baxley and Beebe Hall arrived together. They looked over the valets, and each took an arm of the one they both thought was the best looking and most fit. The other ladies followed protocol.

Everyone was impressed with Mrs. Molly McCurdle's gazebo, the beautiful sterling silver, bone china tea sets, delicious-looking linens, and the lovely, nosegay bouquets that were on the tables.

No one was impressed with the meager amount of alcohol served in the gazebo. Mrs. Charles Chatterton whispered to Mrs. Stanley Bigsbee, "Oh dear, if I would have known this, we would have had a couple more before we came. I feel like we're at a Sunday School picnic." Mrs. Stanley Bigsbee winked back at her friend, opened her handbag, and handed her a small bottle of whiskey to shore up her drink. She whispered back, "You got to think like a Boy Scout and always be prepared."

Bunny Baxley and Beebe Hall had no problems. They always carried little bottles in their handbags for occasions like today. They had been caught empty-handed once before, and vowed never again. Most of the other ladies had pharmaceuticals to get them through the drought.

The Gazebo Party was too perfectly orchestrated, too dry, (in more than one way) and too boring for most of the ladies on The Executives' Wives' Cookbook Committee. Towards the end of the party, Mrs. Molly McCurdle's chitter-chatter and exaggerated charm was getting on everyone's nerves, except for Mrs. E.O. Bittleduke and Mrs. Michael Stellar. They ignored her ramblings, and enjoyed all the beauty, butterflies, and bees.

In their minds they all knew that Mrs. Molly McCurdle meant well, but like Maribelle Biche said to

Mrs. Elmer Steele, as they were leaving, "All her syrupy sweet talk drove me crazy. She buzzes like a bunch of honey bees drinking nectar. Only she doesn't know when to leave the flower, or how to go for the sting."

Mrs. Molly McCurdle was exhausted when the day was over. She couldn't wait until dusk when she could become Mary Poppins or Cinderella, or just practice her ballet routine. The Lawnboy cleaned up, and had to tell her that one of her Francis I sterling silver knives was missing.

Strawberry Julep with Mint

32 large strawberries, cleaned and hulled

1 cup sugar
1 cup water
fresh mint sprigs
crushed ice
1 quart very fine Kentucky bourbon

Refrigerate strawberries. Boil the sugar and water for approximately 4-5 minutes. Place sugar/water mixture in a covered container and add 4-5 sprigs of mint. Refrigerate overnight.

The next day, crush 16 strawberries and spoon strawberry mixture into 16 silver julep cups. Fill the julep cup with crushed ice; then add 1 tablespoon of sugar/water/mint syrup and 2 ounces of Kentucky bourbon. Stir vigorously with a silver spoon so that the outside of the julep cup becomes frosty. Garnish with a fresh sprig of mint and 1 large strawberry that has been cut into slices. This recipe makes 16 juleps.

Even though most of the ladies raved about the Strawberry Juleps, they all thought the drinks were weak and needed more bourbon.

Chilled, Cucumber Soup with Cream Sherry & Rose Petals

5 large seeded cucumbers, peeled & sliced
2 teaspoons salt
1 teaspoon white pepper
2 teaspoons fresh dill weed, chopped
2 green onions, chopped finely
4 tablespoons lemon juice, freshly squeezed
1 ½ cups sour cream
½ cup vanilla yogurt
½ cup cream sherry

washed rose petals

In a blender, blend all ingredients except rose petals. Chill for several hours. Pour soup into soup tureen, and garnish with washed rose petals.

Upon seeing the soup, Mrs. Michael Stellar said, "It's so beautiful, it looks like butterfly nectar." She didn't eat it though.

Wilted, Dandelion Salad with Nasturtium & Violets

2 pounds dandelion greens, washed, chopped and dried

1 pound bacon
¾ cup red wine vinegar
1 tablespoon salt
1 teaspoon pepper
1 teaspoon parsley, chopped finely

nasturtium & violet flowers for garnish

Wash, chop and dry the dandelion greens. Gently arrange dandelion greens in bowl. Fry the bacon and cut into small pieces. Drain. Add vinegar, salt, pepper and parsley to the bacon. Pour the bacon/vinegar/spice mixture over the dandelion greens. Toss gently and garnish with nasturtium and violet flowers.

Most of the ladies had made up their minds not to eat the dandelion salad until Mrs. Christina Pebbleworth-Stafford, acting like 'Miss know-it-all', said that dandelions were used in France all the time because they are a natural diuretic, appetite suppressant and helped with liver problems. Bunny's ears perked up when she heard of the medicinal properties of dandelions, but she still could not get herself to eat 'green food,' healthy or not.

Lemon Loaf

¾ cup butter
1 ½ cups sugar
3 eggs
2 ¼ cups flour, sifted
¼ teaspoon salt
¼ teaspoon baking soda
¾ cup buttermilk
1 lemon

Glaze
2 lemons
¾ cup sugar

Cream the butter and sugar. Beat in eggs, one at a time. Sift flour, salt and baking soda together, and add to batter, alternating with milk. Mix well. Stir in rind of 1 grated lemon. Pour this mixture into a greased and floured 9x5x3 inch pan. Bake at 325° for 1 hour, or until a cake tester comes out clean.

Cool lemon loaf in pan for 15 minutes. Remove lemon loaf from pan, and cover it with a glaze made of the juice of 2 lemons and ½ cup sugar.

For Mrs. Molly McCurdle, food was all about color and looking pretty. This lemon loaf 'fit the bill.'

Asparagus Soufflé

⅓ cup butter
3 tablespoons flour
1 cup half and half
4 eggs, separated
1 teaspoon salt
1 teaspoon white pepper

2 cups asparagus

2 cups asparagus tips

In a saucepan, melt butter. Add the flour, and stir constantly. When the mixture is creamy smooth, slowly add the half and half and stir until thickened. Remove from heat. Cool. Add 4 beaten egg yolks, salt and white pepper to mixture. Gingerly fold in 4 stiffly beaten egg whites.

Grease a soufflé dish and add two cups of asparagus to the bottom of the dish. Gently pour the mixture over the asparagus. Bake at 375° for 35-45 minutes, or until puffy and slightly browned. Garnish with asparagus tips.

To most of the ladies, the asparagus soufflé looked lovely and tasted likewise. However, Bunny Baxley looked at it, wrinkled up her nose, and with her hand to the side of her mouth, said to Beebe Hall, "Ugh, more green food. Even Fifi wouldn't touch this. It looks like something rabbits would eat." Beebe Hall whispered back, "Maybe Doris Dupré will ask for a 'Bunny Bag.' "

Summer Fruit Cake

½ cup butter
⅔ cup sugar
6 egg whites
1 cup pecans, chopped
½ cup slivered almonds
½ cup raisins
½ cup candied cherries
½ cup candied pineapple

1 teaspoon almond extract
¾ teaspoon vanilla extract

1 ¾ cup cake flour, sifted
1 teaspoon baking powder

Preheat oven to 300°. Cream the butter, and slowly add the sugar. Cream until mixture is buttery and fluffy. Add the egg whites, one at a time and beat thoroughly. Mix in nuts, raisins, candied fruit and extracts. In separate bowl, mix the sifted cake flour and baking powder. Slowly add the flour mixture to the butter/cream mixture. Pour into a greased 8x4x3 inch pan. Bake at 300° for about 1 hour and 20 minutes. This recipe serves 10-12 people.

Everyone knew nobody ever ate fruit cake, and that Mrs. Molly McCurdle made it for the simple reason it was pink-colored. When Maribelle Biche realized that Mrs. Molly McCurdle was serving fruit cake, she whispered to Mrs. Grant Goldman-Hues, "What a waste."

Petticoat Tails

½ cup butter, softened
½ cup powdered sugar
¼ teaspoon almond extract
¼ teaspoon vanilla extract
1 cup flour
dash of salt

Cream the butter and shortening. Add the almond and vanilla extract and mix. Stir in flour, mix, and roll into a ball. Roll out mixture to pie crust thickness and cut into triangular shapes. Place them on a greased cookie sheet. Bake at 350° for 10-15 minutes, or until slightly brown. This recipe makes about 3 dozen small petticoat tails.

Mrs. Molly McCurdle made these Scottish cookies as a way to console Mrs. Elmer Steele. She knew that nothing was going right for the poor dear.

Lollipops

1 cup sugar
½ cup water
¼ teaspoon salt
⅓ cup light corn syrup

¼ teaspoon peppermint flavoring
1 drop of red food coloring

In a saucepan, combine sugar, salt, water and corn syrup; stir until the sugar has dissolved. Slowly bring to a boil. Using a candy thermometer, boil the mixture until the temperature reaches 275°. Lower the temperature on the stove, and cook until the mixture reaches a temperature of 300°. Add the peppermint flavoring, food coloring and stir. Pour mixture into greased cupcake tins, and place a paper lollipop stick in the middle of each lollipop round. Allow to harden approximately 5 to 10 minutes. Remove lollipops from cupcake tins and wrap in paper. This recipe makes a dozen lollipops.

Shirley Temples

1 large can of Hi-C fruit punch,
1 large can of pineapple juice
ginger ale
½ bottle grenadine
ice

Pour Hi-C fruit punch, pineapple juice, ginger ale and grenadine in a punch bowl. Add lots of ice, and pansy flowers to float. Serve in dainty cups.

Right before everyone was leaving, Mrs. Molly McCurdle brought out the lollipops on a silver tray. She had The Lawnboy bring out the punch bowl and 'try' to serve the ladies. Most of them politely said, "No-thank-you." When she ran into her home to get the napkins she had forgotten to bring out, Katrina Canfield shook her head and said audibly, "You've got to be kidding. Where in the world does this lady come from?" Bunny Baxley, not being one to miss a beat, stood up, and started singing "Lollipop, Lollipop, Oh Lolli-Lollipop," etc. She put her index finger into the side of her check in her mouth, and pulling her finger out she made the 'pop' sound. Everyone, except Martha Payne and Doris Dupré politely laughed when they heard the loud 'pop' sound. Martha Payne quickly left and Doris Dupré jumped.

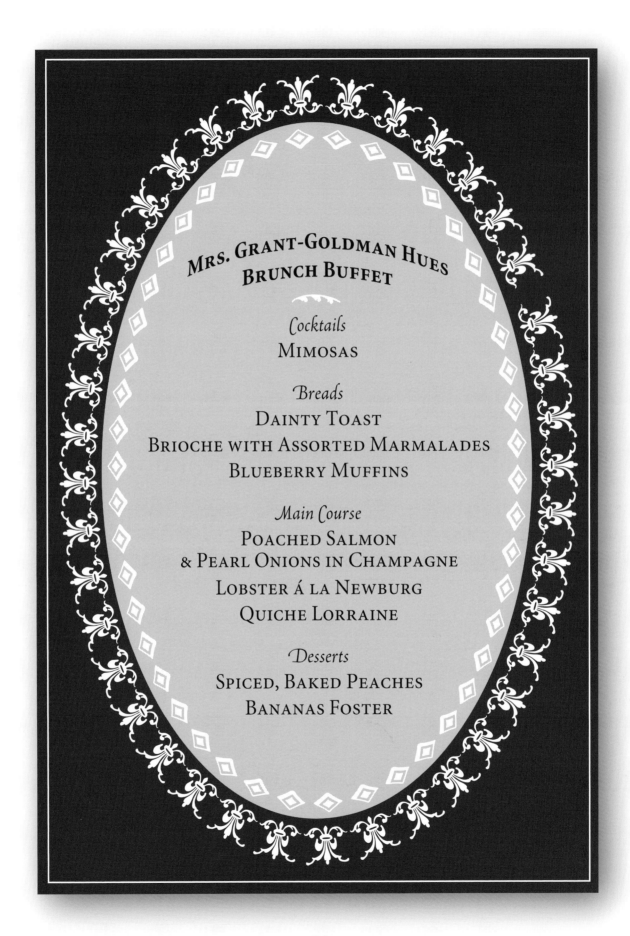

Mrs. Grant-Goldman Hues
Brunch Buffet

Cocktails
Mimosas

Breads
Dainty Toast
Brioche with Assorted Marmalades
Blueberry Muffins

Main Course
Poached Salmon
& Pearl Onions in Champagne
Lobster á la Newburg
Quiche Lorraine

Desserts
Spiced, Baked Peaches
Bananas Foster

MRS. GRANT GOLDMAN-HUES' BRUNCH BUFFET

Whether she is playing chess, hosting her yearly brunch for The Executives' Wives' Cookbook Committee, or donned in her dazzling diamonds, Mrs. Grant Goldman-Hues isn't satisfied unless she knows in her mind that what she does, and what she has, is the best.

When The Executives' Wives' Cookbook Committee comes to her home for her annual brunch, they know her food is more than delectable, it is a masterpiece. Mrs. Goldman-Hues, or Harriett Helen, as only her most intimate and dearest friends are privileged to call her, believes that presentation is everything, and she leaves no stones unturned when it comes to entertaining, down to the perfectly shaped bouquets of small white dahlias that are clustered in silver vases on tables and side tables in every room.

Mrs. Goldman-Hues' collection of sterling silver chafing dishes, silverware, and serving dishes would make anybody green with envy, and it does have that affect on some.[39]

Everyone on The Executives' Wives' Cookbook Committee made a concerted effort to be at Mrs. Goldman-Hues' brunch because everyone knew how hard she worked to make everything, including herself, look beautiful, glorious and charming.

Mrs. Goldman-Hues enjoys entertaining, but secretly gets irritated when it comes to the *Mia Culpas* of her friends. Katrina Canfield always tries her best to 'out dress' everyone, and Bunny Baxley and Martha Payne always come unfashionably late. Mrs. Stanley Bigsbee and Mrs. Charles Chatterton invariably leave indelible lipstick marks on her fine, linen napkins. Beebe Hall is always fiddling with sternos under the chafing dishes; and Maribelle Biche always asks for her recipes.[40]

After one of her infamous brunches, her caterer brought to her attention that her rare, sterling silver marmalade spoon with the rabbit-embossed handle was missing. After that episode her suspicions were aroused and she made an effort to nonchalantly watch everyone more closely.[41]

As usual, Mrs. Grant Goldman-Hues was exhausted after her annual brunch. Instructing The Lawnboy, her caterer and his staff on how to clean and store all her silver was such a chore. However, she is so confident that her brunch was, as usual, so lovely and so successful, that the ladies of The Executives' Wives' Cookbook Committee would be talking about it for a long time.

Mimosas

4 cups of champagne, chilled
1 cup of fresh orange juice, chilled

Mix together and pour into glasses.

Mrs. Grant Goldman-Hues liked to serve Mimosas because they were easy to make, easy to refill, and, looked and tasted refreshing. Sometimes she garnished them with fresh, edible flowers. Bunny Baxley once told Mrs. Grant Goldman-Hues that you can drink Mimosas as early in the morning as you wish because the Vitamin C in the orange juice handles lots of problems. Bunny Baxley elaborated, "I know what's healthy. Just ask me." Mrs. Grant Goldman-Hues didn't answer her.

Brioche Bread

Brioche Bread is something you buy from your favorite bakery or you have your trusted caterer get it for you. Be sure you taste it before you serve it to your guests so you can be reassured it is up to your standards. Serve the bread with a variety of high-quality marmalades. Three different

---

[39] *Mrs. Samuel Squire, Mrs. E.O. Bittleduke, Mrs. Michael Stellar and Mrs. Jonathan Hurlinger are usually not envious, but, like everyone else, they're not perfect. At least they are subtle about it, not like Mrs. Christina Pebbleworth-Stafford who is obviously tarnished with envy.*

[40] *Mrs. Grant Goldman-Hues has always felt that her recipes are like her personal gems. They belong to her, and were hers alone. No two are alike, and you never ever want someone else to have one that is remotely similar. She always told Maribelle Biche that the caterer owns the recipes, and she is not privileged to divulge his secrets.*

[41] *She had a hunch Doris Dupré was the culprit. It was only a hunch, but a strong hunch nevertheless.*

marmalades that Mrs. Grant Goldman-Hues decided to serve at this luncheon were: peach, orange-cranberry and lemon. The colors of the marmalade were luscious and played off each other in her antique, silver, divided marmalade dish.

Blueberry Muffins

2 cups flour, sifted
½ cup sugar
¾   teaspoon salt
2 ½ teaspoons baking powder

¼ cup shortening
1 egg
1 cup milk
1 teaspoon pure vanilla

1 cup of blueberries

In mixing bowl, sift flour and combine it with sugar, salt and baking powder. In a separate mixing bowl, mix shortening, eggs, milk, and vanilla together. Combine the flour mixture with the shortening/egg/milk mixture, stirring until everything is blended. Slowly add 1 cup of blueberries. Spoon the mixture into paper-lined muffin tins. Bake for 20 to 25 minutes at 400°. This recipe makes twelve muffins.

Mrs. Grant Goldman-Hues puts her blueberry muffins on a beautiful, silver tray that is edged with blueberries. She doesn't eat blueberries, but they remind her of sapphires.

Poached Salmon & Pearl Onions in Champagne

4-5 cups of champagne
1 small jar of pearl onions
2 tablespoons soft butter
4 dill sprigs
1 teaspoon salt
1 teaspoon pepper

4 wild salmon fillets
3 tablespoons fresh dill, finely minced

Combine champagne, pearl onions, butter, dill, salt, and pepper in a sauté pan and par boil. Simmer for about 8 minutes. Gently add the salmon fillets, and

spoon the boiled mixture over the salmon. Do this until the salmon is cooked through and firm. Depending upon the thickness of the salmon fillets, this takes about 6-7 minutes. Do not overcook. Pour the liquid mixture into a chafing dish and gently add the fillets. Sprinkle with more fresh dill.

Mrs. Grant Goldman-Hues made twelve fillets, or three batches. The pearl onions are her personal touch. She feels they are so opulent-looking, she could string them. They remind her of richness without the calories. Besides, she knows she needs a vegetable to make her brunch well-rounded. She also adds more fresh dill after everything is in the chafing dish. It just looks richer.

Lobster á la Newburg

1 stick of butter, plus 1 teaspoon
2 teaspoons salt
1 teaspoon black pepper
1 teaspoon cayenne pepper
¼ cup cognac
4 cups of raw lobster meat

⅔ cup of cream
yolks of 4 eggs
½ cup sherry

Melt the butter. Add salt, black pepper, cayenne pepper and sauté the lobster in this mixture. Heat the cognac and pour it over the lobster. Cook for three to four minutes. Set aside.
Beat the egg yolks and add cream. Add the egg yolk/cream mixture to the lobster mixture. Stir until everything is well-blended and slightly thickened. Add ½ cup of sherry. Put in chafing dish and serve on small toasts.

Mrs. Grant Goldman-Hues always serves lobster dishes. Nobody really eats them because they're too rich. The only reason she serves them is because they look rich. Invariably Maribelle Biche asks for the leftovers for her cat.

Quiche Lorraine

1 unbaked pastry shell

6 slices bacon
1 cup yellow onion, finely chopped

4 eggs

1 ¾ cup light cream

1 teaspoon salt

½ teaspoon pepper

¼ teaspoon ground nutmeg

1 cup Swiss cheese, finely shredded

Fry bacon, drain, crumble, and set aside on paper towel. Chop onion. In a mixing bowl, combine eggs, cream, salt, pepper, nutmeg, and beat. Put the unbaked pastry shell in a pretty, quiche baking dish. Arrange bacon and onion on the bottom of the pastry shell. Then add the Swiss cheese on top of bacon/onion combination. Pour egg/cream/seasoning mixture into the shell. Bake at 350° for thirty minutes, or until a knife comes out clean.

She didn't give us the recipe for the pastry shell. She made it well-known that ladies like her don't roll dough. According to her, the only logical choice a person like her has is to have a catering staff make it, or buy it.

Mrs. Grant Goldman-Hues didn't want to serve Quiche Lorraine, but she felt an obligation. Mrs. Michael Stellar and Mrs. E.O. Bittleduke had graciously asked her to be the First Vice President of the Butterfly Ball and she accepted the obligation. As a token of their appreciation, they presented her with a very expensive Spode quiche dish. She didn't like it because it wasn't suited to her taste, and it didn't fit in with any of her décor. However, she felt an obligation to use it at a time when they could see that she was actually using it, thus giving the impression that she liked and appreciated it. She detests playing this game, but she knows she must.

Spiced, Baked Peaches

12 peaches, peeled and halved

2 cups brown sugar

½ teaspoon cinnamon, ground

¼ teaspoon nutmeg

2 teaspoons cloves

1 ½ cups water

1 cup bourbon

1 pint whipping cream

½ cup sugar

1 teaspoon pure vanilla

Arrange the peaches on the bottom of a baking dish. Boil brown sugar, cinnamon, nutmeg and cloves in water for 6 minutes. Pour the boiled mixture over the peaches. Bake at 375° for approximately 25 minutes. Take the baking pan out of the oven and pour the bourbon over the peaches. Bake for 3 to 4 more minutes. Transfer peaches and juice to a chafing dish. Whip the cream with sugar and vanilla. Place a pretty bowl filled with whipping cream on the side of the chafing dish so your guests can indulge in as much cream as they want.

The cream was a waste. Nobody took any.

Bananas Foster

6 firm bananas, sliced into quarters

3 tablespoons butter, softened

6 tablespoons brown sugar

1 teaspoon cinnamon

½ teaspoon nutmeg

¼ cup brandy

¼ cup dark rum

¼ cup white rum

¼ cup banana flavored liqueur

½ gallon French vanilla ice cream

Melt the butter in a chafing dish. Add cinnamon and nutmeg to brown sugar and put the sugar/spices mixture into the melted butter. Stir and blend. Carefully add the bananas. When the bananas are soft, pour the brandy, dark rum, white rum and banana flavored liqueur over the mixture and ignite. Serve with French vanilla ice cream.

When the caterer was igniting the Bananas Foster, Beebe Hall was standing right in front of him. It was obvious to everyone that she was in his way. One of the caterers cleared his throat as a signal to let Beebe Hall know that she should move, but in her excitement she had no clue what he was doing, and stood her territory. Mrs. Grant Goldman-Hues saw it but didn't say anything. She felt that she was paying 'good' money for the caterer and the staff to handle everything, and it was their duty to figure it out. As she and her friends always lamented, "It's so tough to get good help nowadays."

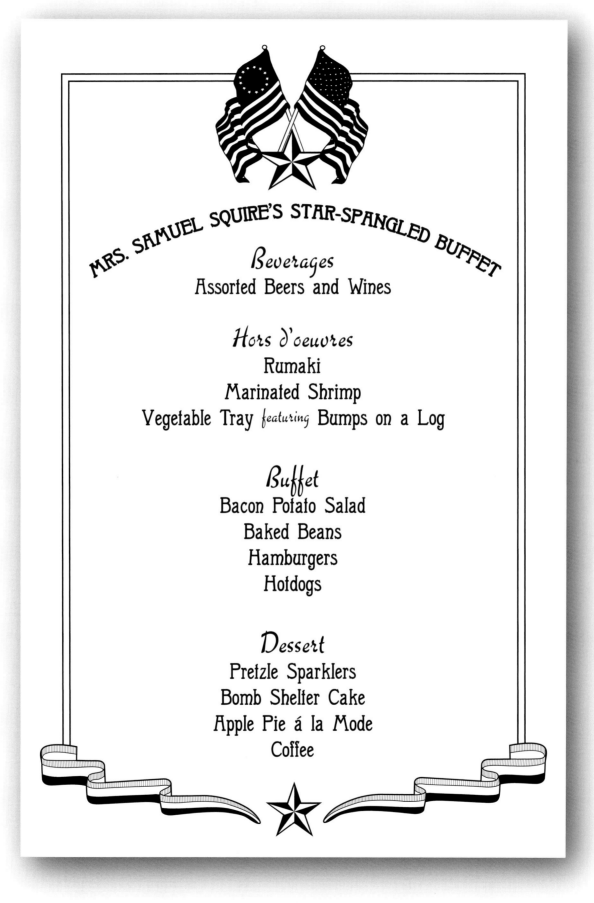

MRS. SAMUEL SQUIRE'S STAR-SPANGLED BUFFET

Beverages
Assorted Beers and Wines

Hors d'oeuvres
Rumaki

Marinated Shrimp

Vegetable Tray *featuring* Bumps on a Log

Buffet
Bacon Potato Salad

Baked Beans

Hamburgers

Hotdogs

Dessert
Pretzle Sparklers

Bomb Shelter Cake

Apple Pie á la Mode

Coffee

THE SQUIRE'S SNAP, CRACKLE AND POP 4TH OF JULY

Immediately after Memorial Day or Decoration Day as Mr. Samuel Squire has always called it, the Squires start planning their annual 4th of July extravaganza that they have hosted every year since they were married. Mrs. Samuel Squire would just as soon be on holiday as to host a 4th of July celebration every year, but she knows Samuel's in his glory when flying Old Glory on what he has told everyone is 'the most important day of the year.'

The work they have always put into their 4th of July celebrations is something nobody else would care to do. With Mr. Samuel Squire, overseeing the outside work, and Mrs. Squire handling the details inside the home, they have always worked like a military drill team in synchronized harmony. Mrs. Samuel Squire never told her husband, but did tell Mrs. E.O. Bittleduke, that even though she knows that planning for the 4th of July has always been her husband's passion, his patriotic 'hymn humming' drives her nuts.

Usually they invite their Republican cohorts, and their blue-blood friends who are members of the same historical, exclusive and prestigious organizations that help to promote and preserve their celebration. This year their guest list was different and so was the party. Mrs. Samuel Squire invited the members of The Executives' Wives' Cookbook Committee because she thought it would be a perfect time for her to showcase her recipes for the cookbook. Mr. Samuel Squire thought it was important that they serve what they always serve, food he refers to as 'American heartland' food. He said to his wife, "Boys from all walks of life gave their life for our liberty. Most of them didn't grow up eating French food." "Besides," he continued, "even though France has been our ally, I don't think it was necessary for Jackie Kennedy to bring over a French Chef, and I don't think they have thanked us properly for the Statue of Liberty, so we need to honor what our celebration is all about." He kept rambling. "You know that Kennedy stole the election. If you have to serve foreign food, I think it should be food dishes that are unique to England and to honor Winston Churchill, and what he did for the world." She stopped him and said, "Enough said. We will serve

what we have always served." However, deep down she was somewhat embarrassed, and regretted it for years to come.

There were only ten of The Executives' Wives' Cookbook Committee that could make it to the celebration, but with their spouses that was twenty, and that was more than enough for Mrs. Samuel Squire. She couldn't wait until the day was over. Mr. Samuel Squire, on the other hand, was so excited he didn't sleep a wink the night before the party. Early in the morning he was out surveying the grounds to make sure his 'flag flower garden 'was perfectly manicured and there were no spent blossoms on the flowers. He had requested his flag staff, as well as the fireworks team, be on duty two hours before the guests were to arrive. The Lawnboy, who he had hired to be the bartender, was also to report two hours before the party, and he did. The caterers had set up the big white tents the night before, so everything would be ready.

When the guests arrived, they were greeted by patriotic hymns blaring out of speakers that were positioned in trees. Mr. Squire greeted everyone, handed everyone a small flag, told them to get a drink and encouraged them to go inside to see his historical flag displays. Everyone got a drink, but only the Bittledukes, Steeles, Biches, Duprés, Paynes and McCurdles went inside to see the flags. As Bunny Baxley told Beebe Hall when she was going for her second drink, "You've seen one flag, you've seen them all." After the guests, who were gracious enough to go see the flags, went outside Mrs. Molly McCurdle said to Mr. Samuel Squire, "Where's the Confederate Flag?" Before Mr. Samuel Squire could start on another history lesson, Mr. Kent McCurdle intervened and led his wife away.

After Mr. Samuel Squire had requested that everyone be seated, he asked them to stand up and recite the Pledge of Allegiance. Everyone could see that Mrs. Samuel Squire was embarrassed by her husband's request, and no one was more miffed than Mrs. Elmer Steele when she saw that Bunny Baxley couldn't recite the words to the Pledge of Allegiance, and Beebe Hall was laughing at Bunny's inability to recite.

Martha Payne, who had done everything in her power to muster the courage to show up, surprised everyone by how loud she was speaking, but nobody knew she had cotton in her ears to protect her from the sounds of the fireworks and other loud sounds that frightened her.

Mrs. Christina Pebbleworth-Stafford was mortified when she saw what the Squires were serving. She said to Mrs. E.O. Bittleduke, "I can't believe they're serving peasant food. Our palettes don't allow us to eat this kind of food. To think I've wasted a 4th of July holiday and now, where are we going to get reservations at this time of the day?" They left before Mrs. E.O. Bittleduke, who didn't think Mrs. Christina Pebbleworth-Stafford was acting gracious, could respond. Mrs. Samuel Squire saw them leave and was furious.

After the meal, and before the fireworks, most of the guests were bored out of their minds and some of them just kept drinking. As the twilight hour was coming on, things started to 'pick up,' as Bunny Baxley called it. Before anyone realized it, both Mrs. Charles Chatterton and Dr. E.O. Bittleduke had wandered off, and, as usual, the hunt was on for them. Much to Mrs. E.O. Bittleduke's horror she found them in the car. With the engine manual in hand, he was talking to Mrs. Charles Chatterton who didn't hear him because she was passed out in the back seat. When she approached the window to the car, he looked at her and said, "Nurse, I'll be with you in a minute. I have a patient in the recovery room." When Mrs. E.O. Bittleduke told her husband to move over to the passenger side, Mrs. Chatterton woke up and said, "Doctor, all I need is my pills, and I'll be fine." Mrs. E.O. Bittleduke asked Mr. Elmer Steele who had gone with her on 'the hunt' to guide Mrs. Charles Chatterton back to the party. Dr. and Mrs. E.O. Bittleduke left before anyone knew what had happened.

In the meantime, Mrs. Stanley Bigsbee hired herself to help The Lawnboy mix drinks. After she spilled more liquor on the floor than in the glasses, The Lawnboy guided her back to a chair. She said, "Oh you cutie, little button, I will have to tell Elizabeth about you again." Mr. Elmer Squire, oblivious to what 'state

of mind' Mrs. Chatterton and Mrs. Bigsbee were in, handed each of them a sparkler. Immediately both of them thought the sparklers were cigarettes, and they both tried to light them. Both Mr. Chatterton and Mr. Bigsbee saw it, took the sparklers from their wives and knew it was time to go home. They guided their wives back to their cars before the 'real fireworks' started.

At this point in the party, Beebe Hall and Bunny Baxley decided they needed to start their own fireworks. Beebe Hall, who had asked The Lawnboy to make her and Bunny Baxley some *Sambucas* decided it was time 'for show and tell.' Beebe Hall lit the *Sambucas*, and Bunny Baxley, who was already 'lit' started to juggle the *Sambucas*. Mrs. Samuel Squire, who was used to calm and proper guests, went inside hoping everyone would just leave.

Mr. Samuel Squire, oblivious to everything except flags, fireworks and apple pie, told everyone to sit down because his fireworks show would be starting shortly. Beebe Hall and Bunny Baxley decided that they were going to watch it from the Squires' garage roof. After they got on top of the roof, they had a bird's eye view of what was actually happening. Mr. Elmer Steele was behind a tree with a lady they couldn't recognize, Mrs. Elmer Steele was still eating, and the Biches were sitting like statues staring out into space. They saw Klog Dupré up in a tree, and Doris Dupré running through the bushes, sling shot in hand shooting rabbits with stones. Beebe Hall said to Bunny Baxley, "She looks like Davy Crockett. When she rounds the corner, let's spit some watermelon seeds at her and watch her jump."

When Beebe Hall and Bunny Baxley's husbands saw that their wives were on top of the roof, they went up and brought them down. Their husbands wanted to go, but they knew the ladies, especially Beebe Hall, would want to watch the fireworks. The Biches left. She said to her husband, "Let's go. She doesn't have a recipe I would care to have." Nobody knew if the Duprés left or if they stayed in the woods all night, but they weren't anywhere to be seen when the fireworks started.

Mr. Samuel Squire, narrated the fireworks show, and only the Halls, the Baxleys, The Lawnboy and the caterers were there to watch it. Everyone, including

The Lawnboy, was drunk. It didn't seem to bother Mr. Samuel Squire. He just needed to see the American flag, his red, white and blue, light up in the sky. *Postscript: When Mr. Samuel Squire was putting his flag away the next day, he was distraught that one of them was missing. He said to his wife, "Nothing like this ever happened when we entertained our Republican friends."*

Rumaki

2 pounds chicken livers
24 slices bacon strips, cut in half
24 ounces chicken livers, halved
24 water chestnuts, halved

Marinade
½ cup soy sauce
2 teaspoons ginger, minced
4 tablespoons dry sherry
2 teaspoons sugar

Combine soy sauce, ginger, sherry and sugar in a bowl. Add the chicken livers and water chestnut pieces and marinate them in the refrigerator for 1 hour. Wrap the bacon around the chicken liver and water chestnut. Secure with a toothpick.

Place the *Rumaki* in a shallow baking pan and bake at 375° for 20-25 minutes. Serve the *Rumaki* hot.

Marinated Shrimp

10 pounds shrimp, steamed and peeled
2 purple onions, sliced into rings
2 small jars capers
chopped parsley

Marinade
2 cups olive oil
1 ½ cups white vinegar
3 tablespoons Worcestershire sauce
2 tablespoons Tabasco sauce
4 teaspoons sugar
4 teaspoons salt
1 teaspoon white pepper
½ teaspoon cayenne pepper

Place shrimp, onion rings and capers in a large,

shallow container. Combine marinade ingredients and pour over shrimp. Refrigerate for 24 hours, stirring occasionally. Garnish with chopped parsley.

With her plate and mouth full of food, Mrs. Elmer Steele said to anyone within ear shot, "I'm disappointed with her appetizers. You think she would have come up with something more creative."

Vegetable Tray
Featuring Bumps on a Log

Mrs. Samuel Squire always made Bumps on a Log for her grandchildren. She thought some of the ladies, who were always on a diet and grabbed for the celery sticks, would get some nutrition from the peanut butter and raisins.

Baked Beans

4 cans pork and beans (4 pounds)
1 ½ cups brown sugar
2 teaspoons prepared mustard

12 strips bacon, chopped finely
1 cup catsup

Mix all the ingredients together and bake uncovered for 3 hours at 325°.

Maribelle Biche looked at the beans, shook her head, and said "Food like this? – for the ladies of The Executives' Wives' Cookbook Committee? What is she thinking?"

Bacon Potato Salad

18 potatoes
½ pound bacon
½ cup shallots, finely chopped
½ cup red wine vinegar
4 tablespoons olive oil
1 teaspoon prepared mustard
2 teaspoons salt
1 teaspoon pepper
1 cup chopped parsley

Chop the bacon and sauté in a skillet until crisp. Dry the bacon on paper towels. In the bacon fat, sauté the chopped shallots until they are tender.
Peel the potatoes and boil them until they are tender, but firm. Pour vinegar, olive oil, prepared mustard, shallots and the bacon fat over the hot potatoes. Season with salt and pepper, add the parsley and toss. Cool the potato salad to room temperature, cover and refrigerate. If the potato salad seems dry, add some more olive oil and vinegar.

Upon seeing the potato salad, Mrs. Charles Chatterton whispered to Mrs. Stanley Bigsbee, "This looks like school cafeteria food."

Hamburgers and Hotdogs

When grilling hamburgers and hotdogs, use the best meat available, and ask your guests how they would like them prepared.

When the caterer asked Martha Payne if she wanted her hamburger rare, medium or well-down, she said, "Raw please."

Pretzel Sparklers

1 bag of pretzel rods
1 bag of white, chocolate morsels or 1 bag of large marshmallows
red and blue sprinkles

Melt the white chocolate morsels or the bag of marshmallows in a double boiler. Immediately dip the pretzel rods halfway into the melted chocolate or melted marshmallows. Dip each one in red and blue sprinkles. Stand the pretzels upright in a tall cup or glass until they are dry. Tie the ends of the pretzels with red, white and blue ribbon.

Beebe Hall and Bunny Baxley tried to light these; then they switched to Pall Malls.

Bomb Shelter Cake

1 package devil's food cake mix
1 can cherry pie filling
1 teaspoon almond extract
1 pint whipping cream
Maraschino cherries and blueberries for garnish

Prepare and bake two 8 inch layers of cake from a devil's food cake mix. Cool the cakes on wire racks. Whip the cream until it is stiff. Add 1 teaspoon of almond extract. Fold in a can of cherry pie filling. Do not drain the can. Place one of the 8 inch layers on a glass cake plate. Frost the cake with the cherry pie filling/whipped cream mixture. Place the second cake on top of first one. Spread the rest of the cherry/whipping cream mixture on the top and sides of the cake. Garnish with maraschino cherries and blueberries. Garnish with miniature toothpick flags. Chill until served.

Mr. Samuel Squire always joked, "If the Communists force you into your bomb shelter, this cake will bring a lot of comfort." Nobody could understand what he meant by it, or even tried to understand him. He was always rambling on about things that never made any sense.

Apple Pie á la Mode

Crust for two pies

3 cups flour
1 teaspoon salt
1 tablespoon vinegar
1 ¼ cups shortening
5 tablespoons water
1 egg, beaten well

Sift flour and salt together, cut in shortening. Mix egg, water and vinegar. Add to the flour mixture. Roll out between wax paper.

Pie filling

⅔ cup brown sugar
⅔ cup white sugar
2 tablespoons flour
2 teaspoons lemon juice
1 teaspoon cinnamon
½ teaspoon nutmeg
15 cups apples, peeled, cored and sliced
1 egg
sugar to sprinkle

Combine the pie filling ingredients in a large bowl, mixing well so all apples are covered with sugar mixture. Spoon the apple mixture into the two prepared pie shells. Top each pie with the remaining rolled out crusts. Crimp edges of both top and bottom crusts together. Give the top of each pie an egg wash of an egg beaten with 2 teaspoons water. Divide evenly. Sprinkle with sugar. Bake at 350° for 40-60 minutes or until golden brown. Serve the pie with vanilla ice cream.

This recipe was given to the Squires by Mr. Squire's mother. She was a fine lady and a good Republican too.

Mrs. Michael Stellar's High Tea

Variety of Teas

Currant Scones with Devonshire Cream and/or Lemon Curd

Minted-Radish Tea Sandwiches

Cucumber Tea Sandwiches

Orange Poppy Seed Bread

English Trifle

High Tea Lemon Cookies

Russian Tea Cakes

Mississippi Belle Black Bottom Pie

MRS. MICHAEL STELLAR'S HIGH TEA - THE STING

As would be expected, the lovely and gracious Mrs. Michael Stellar had orchestrated everything to a 'T' when she hosted The Executives' Wives' Cookbook Committee for a high tea at her beautifully-appointed home. No one knew that the preparation for her high tea event had started months before, and included the restoration of her outdoor antique wrought metal furniture, and the cultivation of a new, grape arbor complete with an antique, French-imported, wrought metal trellis. Because she was nominated to co-chair The Butterfly Ball, she had gone so far as to have her landscaping company plant rose bushes, azaleas, asters, red clover, Queen Ann's Lace, and every other kind of plant that would attract bees and butterflies. The Lawnboy was hired and given explicit instructions on how to properly nurture and take care of the bushes and shrubs.

The care and preparation she took to ensure that every detail was lovely and was well-appreciated by all her guests. Mrs. Michael Stellar, as always, went out of her way to make them all feel welcome, special and important. The table favors, silver, Mint Julep cups monogrammed for each member of The Executives' Wives' Cookbook Committee, were overflowing with baby roses. They all knew her passion and hobby was floral arranging, and with the help of The Lawnboy, they had put the arrangements together with roses that they had picked from her rose garden.

The day of her event was as planned, lovely and inviting. There was only a hint of envy in the air,[42] and Mrs. Michael Stellar had a way of making it dissipate. Martha Payne and Mrs. Molly McCurdle loved to come to the Stellars' home because they knew they wouldn't have to calm 'the butterflies in their stomach' as they often times had to do. Bunny Baxley, Beebe Hall, Mrs. Charles Chatterton and Mrs. Stanley Bigsbee liked the fact that the food portions would be small and dainty, leaving them not having to dream up

excuses for 'wood-pecking'. Mrs. Elmer Steele, on the other hand, knew Mrs. Michael Stellar would be serving an 'out of this world' tasting pie, and her mouth had been watering for weeks in anticipation. Doris Dupré, Mrs. Christina Pebbleworth-Stafford and Katrina Canfield knew that they didn't have to 'have their guard up' at the Stellar's home, thus enabling them to relax. Maribelle Biche was always grateful that Mrs. Michael Stellar graciously shared her recipes. Of course, Mrs. Grant Goldman Hues, Mrs. E.O. Bittleduke and Mrs. Jonathan Hurlinger appreciated loveliness without recourse, and excitedly looked forward to the high tea.

As always, Mrs. Michael Stellar had done everything right to insure a lovely and eventful day, but, unfortunately, there were circumstances beyond her control that turned her high tea into a high-sting highlight that neither she nor anyone in attendance wanted to remember.

After Mrs. Michael Stellar had served her high tea, she, in her southern genteel way, invited everyone out to her gardens to enjoy a Mint Julep.[43] After everyone was seated on her beautiful, wrought metal furniture in her lovely garden which was buzzing with butterflies and bees, The Lawnboy brought out the Mint Juleps on silver trays. Mrs. Michael Stellar gave a lovely toast, the ladies lifted their silver glasses and, like the story of Madame Butterfly, the tragedy began to unfold.

All of a sudden, to everyone's horror, Mrs. Stanley Bigsbee threw her silver Mint Julep cup up in the air and it landed in the grass. Her face turned red as a *roma* tomato, and she jumped up out of her chair. She quickly opened up her purse, grabbed a tissue, and pressed it to her lips. Forgetting to close the clasp on her purse, Mrs. Stanley Bigsbee dropped her purse, and the pills scattered all over the garden.

---

[42] *Mrs. Samuel Squire was obviously miffed that Mrs. Michael Stellar was appointed to host the high tea. She believed with all her heart that she was the obvious choice because of her English lineage. Mrs. Michael Stellar was French, and Mrs. Samuel Squire truly believed that some things are just not imparted properly unless you truly are in the 'blood line.'*

[43] *Bunny Baxley and Beebe Hall, not wanting to hurt this lovely lady's feelings, had brought some little bottles of bourbon in their handbags to embellish the juleps, which they had learned from previous experiences were a 'little weak.'*

At this point, Mrs. Charles Chatterton jumped out of her chair and fell to the ground to gather up the pills. She acted like a child that was scooping up candy thrown by the Shriners at a summer parade.

Mrs. E.O. Bittleduke, who had watched her husband react when he saw trouble, ran over to Mrs. Stanley Bigsbee, pulled the tissue away from her lips and realized that Mrs. Stanley Bigsbee had been stung on her lips by a bee. Everyone looked on in horror when they saw that Mrs. Stanley Bigsbee's lips were swollen up like a blowfish that had been chased by a dolphin. Mrs. E.O. Bittleduke instructed The Lawnboy to get an ice pack, and get one quickly. Before The Lawnboy returned, quick-thinking Bunny Baxley took the ice out of her Mint Julep and put it up to Mrs. Stanley Bigsbee's lips. Thinking it was a popsicle, she started to lick the ice. At this point, the ladies realized that Mrs. Charles Chatterton was out cold on the lawn, her hands were clutched tight, full of pills. Bunny Baxley ran over to Mrs. Charles Chatterton, put an ice cube from her drink on her lips, and she woke up. She looked around, opened her hand, saw the pills and asked for a glass of water. "I need to take my medications," she said. Mrs. E.O. Bittleduke encouraged her to give up the pills and a few of the other ladies helped her sit up in a chair. Beebe Hall lit up an Old Gold for her and she came to her senses, thank goodness.

The Lawnboy was attending to Mrs. Stanley Bigsbee while the others were helping Mrs. Charles Chatterton. Mrs. Stanley Bigsbee asked for a mirror. When she saw her swollen lips she said, "This is the look I've been trying to get my whole life. With lips like this I wouldn't have to color out of the lines. Get me my lipstick."

Everyone laughed and was relieved that she would be okay. Mrs. Michael Stellar, who usually only drank one Mint Julep, asked The Lawnboy to bring out another round of drinks, and she indulged in another one.

When The Lawnboy was cleaning up he had to tell Mrs. Michael Stellar that the silver Mint Julep cup Mrs. Stanley Bigsbee had thrown in the air when she was stung by the bee was nowhere to be found. Mrs. Michael Stellar knew 'through the grapevine' that perhaps Doris Dupré would know, but as everyone knew, she would just as soon buy a new cup as to accuse anyone on The Executives' Wives' Cookbook Committee of taking it. She told The Lawnboy, "Sit down. Let me fix you some lemonade and wait on you." He smiled, and thanked her. She had always been one of his favorites.

Currant Scones

2 cups all-purpose flour
4 tablespoons sugar
2 teaspoons baking powder
¼ teaspoon baking soda
⅛ teaspoon salt
⅓ cup unsalted butter
1 egg
1 teaspoon almond extract
1 cup currants
1 egg, beaten

Combine the flour, sugar, baking powder, baking soda and salt. Cut the butter into the dry mixture until the mixture is of 'course crumb' consistency. Add the egg and almond extract. Knead the dough and roll it into a circle. Cut the dough into circles with a round cookie cutter and place on a cookie sheet. Make an indentation in the center of each scone. Add 1 tablespoon of currants in the indentation. Brush the scone with the beaten egg. Bake at 375° for approximately 15 minutes.

Devonshire Cream

8 ounces cream cheese
4 tablespoons powdered sugar
2 cups whipping cream
2 teaspoons vanilla extract

Blend the cream cheese and powdered sugar. Whip the cream and add the vanilla extract. Fold the cream into the cream cheese. Serve in a small bowl that matches the English bone china plates.

Mrs. Michael Stellar didn't have access to 'real' Devonshire cream, so she made up her own recipe for mock Devonshire cream. Mrs. Samuel Squire, who usually didn't say much, let The Executives' Wives' Cookbook Committee know that it wasn't the 'real' stuff. She said it in a nice way, but got her point across.

Lemon Curd

5 egg yolks
⅓ cup lemon juice, freshly squeezed
¾ cup sugar
4 tablespoons unsalted butter
1 tablespoon lemon zest, finely shredded

In double boiler, whisk together the egg yolks, sugar, and lemon juice until blended. Cook, stirring constantly until the mixture becomes thick. This takes approximately 10 minutes. Remove from heat and immediately pour through a fine strainer to remove any lumps. Cut the butter into small pieces and whisk it into the mixture until the butter has melted. Add the lemon zest and cool.

Just to make a point, Mrs. Samuel Squire ignored the 'mock' Devonshire cream and put the lemon curd on her scone.

Minted-Radish Tea Sandwiches

white-enriched bread, cut into quarters
1 cup mayonnaise
juice of 1 lemon
1 teaspoon salt
1 cup mint leaves, crushed
16 radishes, trimmed and sliced as thin as possible
five radishes made into radish roses

Remove the crust, and cut the bread into quarters. Combine mayonnaise, lemon juice and salt. Spread the white bread with lemon mayonnaise. Sprinkle the crushed mint leaves on top of the lemon mayonnaise. Top with rows of thinly sliced radishes. Sandwiches may be made two hours ahead and plated on English bone china platters surrounded by radish roses. Wrap in plastic wrap and refrigerate until serving time.

Doris Dupré ate three radish sandwiches, and so did Maribelle Biche. They didn't seem to mind that some of the ladies didn't even get to taste one.

Cucumber Tea Sandwiches

rye bread
8 ounces cream cheese, softened
½ cup mayonnaise
1 teaspoon lemon juice
1 teaspoon lemon pepper
cucumbers, thinly sliced

Remove the crust from the rye bread and cut into small squares. Mix the cream cheese, mayonnaise, lemon juice and lemon pepper. Spread this mixture on the bread and top each piece with a slice of cucumber. Cover with plastic wrap and refrigerate until serving time.

Bunny Baxley took a cucumber sandwich and scraped the cucumbers off it.

Orange Poppy Seed Bread

3 cups flour
1 teaspoon salt
1 ½ teaspoons baking powder
4 tablespoons poppy seeds
3 eggs
1 ½ cups milk
1 ¼ cups vegetable oil
1 teaspoon vanilla flavoring
1 teaspoon almond flavoring

Glaze
1 cup powdered sugar
½ cup orange juice, freshly squeezed
½ teaspoon vanilla extract
½ teaspoon almond extract

In a large bowl combine flour, salt, baking powder, and poppy seeds. Add milk, vegetable oil, and vanilla and almond flavorings. Stir this mixture until the ingredients are moistened. Pour the batter into two greased and floured loaf pans. Bake at 350° for about 1 hour, or until a 'knife inserted comes out clean.' Remove the bread from the loaf pans, and pour a glaze made from a mixture of powdered sugar, orange juice, and vanilla and almond extracts over the bread. Cool before slicing.

Mrs. Elmer Steele asked for some butter for her bread. The rest of the ladies thought 'of all the nerve.'

English Trifle

1 large pound cake
¾ cup sherry
2 pints fresh strawberries, chopped
¼ cup sugar

1-3.5 ounce package vanilla pudding mix
2 cups milk

1 cup heavy whipping cream

12 whole strawberries
12 Maraschino cherries
¼ cup almonds, slivered

Cut the pound cake into small pieces, cover with sherry, and put it into a large, pretty, glass bowl. Slice strawberries, sprinkle them with sugar and put them over the pound cake. Cover this with the vanilla pudding mix. Whip the cream and layer it over the pudding. Garnish with whole strawberries, maraschino cherries and slivered almonds.

Beebe Hall took some trifle and only ate the Maraschino cherries. Ditto with Bunny Baxley.

High Tea Lemon Cookies

2 cups butter
⅔ cup sugar
1 teaspoon lemon zest, grated
¼ teaspoon lemon extract
¼ teaspoon vanilla
2 cups flour

Cream butter, sugar, lemon extract and vanilla extract. Add the flour and mix until a dough forms. Roll the dough into small 1 inch balls and bake at 350° for 15 minutes. Cool.

Frosting

⅓ cup butter, room temperature
1 teaspoon lemon zest, grated
⅔ cup lemon juice, freshly squeezed
4 cups powdered sugar

Combine butter, lemon zest, lemon juice, and powdered sugar and stir vigorously until well mixed. Spread the mixture on the cookies. Serve them on a cut-glass, round plate.

Mrs. Michael Stellar made these especially for Mrs. E.O. Bittleduke because she knew it was one of her favorite cookies.

Russian Tea Cakes

1 cup butter softened
1 cup confectioners' sugar
2 ¼ cups flour
1 tablespoon water
¾ cup pecans, finely chopped
confectioners sugar

In a large bowl, mix the butter until it is soft. Slowly add the confectioners' sugar and gently beat until the mixture is fluffy. Stir in the flour, vanilla and pecans. Roll the mixture into 1 inch balls and bake on a cookie sheet for 12 minutes at 400°. Remove from oven, and roll the balls in a bowl of confectioners' sugar. Serve on a cut glass plate.

The Russian Tea Cakes were good, but they were a little messy. Mrs. Elmer Steele had confectioners' sugar all down the front of her blouse, as did Martha Payne and Mrs. Charles Chatterton. Mrs. Elmer Steele noticed the mess on her blouse, wiped off as much as she could with her napkin and continued eating like nothing had happened. Mrs. Charles Chatterton, who had trouble with petit tremors, didn't notice and nobody brought it to her attention. Martha Payne, upon noticing the confectioners' sugar on her blouse, went to the bathroom and took a pill.

Mississippi Belle Black Bottom Pie

Delicious Pie Crust

3 cups flour
1 teaspoon salt
1 tablespoon vinegar
1 ¼ cups shortening

5 tablespoons water
1 egg, beaten well

Sift flour and salt together; cut in shortening. Mix egg, water and vinegar. Add to the flour mixture. Roll out between wax paper. This recipe makes crusts for two double-crusted pies.

Chocolate bottom layer

½ cup sugar
⅛ teaspoon salt
1 ¼ tablespoons corn starch
4 egg yolks, slightly beaten
2 cups milk, scalded
1 cup or 6 ounces chocolate semi-sweet morsels
½ teaspoon vanilla

Thoroughly combine the sugar, salt and cornstarch in a heavy saucepan. Blend in egg yolks. Gradually add hot milk. Cook over moderate heat, stirring constantly, until mixture coats a metal spoon. Remove from heat. Add the chocolate morsels to one cup of this mixture. Stir until chocolate is melted. Pour chocolate mixture into the baked pie shell. Reserve the remaining cooked mixture for the next layer.

White layer

1 envelope gelatin
¼ cup water
1 teaspoon vanilla
4 egg whites
¼ teaspoon cream of tartar
½ cup sugar

Soften gelatin in water. Add the vanilla. Add to the remaining cooked filling and stir until gelatin is dissolved. If filling has cooled, melt the softened gelatin over hot water, and then add it to the cooked mixture.

Cool. Beat egg whites and cream of tartar until foamy; gradually beat in the sugar, and continue to beat until very stiff. Fold egg white into cooked gelatin mixture. Pour very carefully over the chocolate layer in the pie shell. Chill well. Serve with whipped cream and shaved chocolate.

This pie is lovely with rum flavoring. Instead of 2 cups of milk, use ½ cup light rum and 1 ½ cups milk. Add the rum after custard is removed from heat.

One year Mr. and Mrs. Michael Stellar took a Mississippi river boat cruise on the Delta Queen. The featured dessert one evening was Mississippi Belle Black Bottom Pie. Mrs. Michael Stellar, in her soft-spoken Southern genteel way, asked the chef for the recipe, but to no avail. After dinner, they retired to their room. Mr. Michael Stellar excused himself to go have a cigar. However, his mission was otherwise. He went to the kitchen and paid the chef handsomely for the recipe. His wife was delighted. Maribelle Biche asked for the recipe, but this time Mrs. Michael Stellar stood her ground and said it was a family secret that she swore she wouldn't divulge. Rumor has it that the recipe came from the Mississippi Belle Restaurant in Hastings, Minnesota, and is still, at times, served there.

Footnote: The recipes for the pie crust and the Mississippi Belle Black Bottom Pie were taken from the cookbook, <u>Dining on the Plush, Audrey Reissner's Famous Recipes from The Mississippi Belle</u>. © Copyright 1972

Mrs. E. O. Bittleduke's
ANTIQUE LUNCHEON

Champagne Cocktails

APPETIZERS
Pâté de Foie Gras in Cream Cheese Balls
Quiche Tartlets

SOUP
Oyster Bisque

MAIN COURSE
Tarragon Carrots
Chicken Croquettes

DESSERT
Clove Cake

AFTER LUNCH BEVERAGES
Coffee & Tea

MRS. E.O. BITTLEDUKE'S ANTIQUE LUNCHEON

Mrs. E.O. Bittleduke invited The Executives' Wives' Cookbook Committee to her home for a luncheon to showcase her recipes for them, and as a way to thank them for entrusting her to co-chair the Butterfly Ball with Mrs. Michael Stellar. She was touched and honored that they had confidence in her since they all knew how much time and energy it took for her to watch 'The Doctor.'

Dr. and Mrs. E.O. Bittleduke recently returned from London where they purchased a very rare Sheffield silver service set. She was anxious to show off her purchase to the ladies at her luncheon. After the luncheon, she donned her white gloves, and moving in carefully planned precision, she graciously picked up the silver service set piece by piece so everyone could admire it. They all marveled at how beautiful it was, except for Mrs. Samuel Squire. She was too envious to say anything about it.

To further rub salt into the wounds, Mrs. E.O. Bittleduke served coffee and tea in a silver service set that the Squires had bid on at Sotheby's, but didn't get it because the Bittledukes outbid them. The two couples have had a strained relationship ever since.

Everyone on The Executives' Wives' Cookbook Committee came to Mrs. E.O. Bittleduke's luncheon except Mrs. Christina Pebbleworth-Stafford who was in Paris at a fashion runway show, Doris Dupré who didn't give a bona fide reason as to why she couldn't attend, and Katrina Canfield who said she was in the middle of a massive pool-side renovation. Martha Payne left right after lunch. All she said was that she had an appointment. Mrs. Molly McCurdle left early so she could watch her daughters at ballet class.

Mrs. Charles Chatterton, in her habitual manner, went into a mini trance, but she came out of it before she spilled her champagne cocktail on one of Mrs.

E.O. Bittleduke's favorite antique chairs and before anyone had to take any embarrassing action. Mrs. Samuel Squire tried to look like she was enjoying everything, but everyone could tell she was sulking.

Beebe Hall was mesmerized as she looked at Mrs. E.O. Bittleduke's collection of silver candlestick holders and Bunny Baxley who didn't eat except for a bite of a carrot, but had several glasses of champagne cocktails, flitted around like a butterfly while she was flirting with The Lawnboy. Mrs. Stanley Bigsbee had a bad headache, and had obviously overdosed on pharmaceuticals.

Mrs. Jonathan Hurlinger looked lovely as did Mrs. Michael Stellar. Mrs. Grant Goldman-Hues had on a new cocktail ring and hoping to arouse envy, she was doing everything in her power to show it off, short of telling everyone about it.

Maribelle Biche, in her usual bold manner, asked Mrs. E.O. Bittleduke where she got the recipe for the oyster bisque soup. Mrs. Elmer Steele, in her usual manner, tried to steer the conversation towards the work The Executives' Wives' Cookbook Committee needed to do on their cookbook project.

All in all, the antique luncheon was a huge success. The champagne cocktails were the hit. After it was all over, Mrs. E.O. Bittleduke told the caterers to drop the food off at the shelter. She didn't think it was food that her husband should eat.

The Bittleduke's daughter, Gabriella, who had taken 'The Doctor' out to golf for the day, brought her father home after everyone had left. When it was all over, Mrs. E.O. Bittleduke was relieved, but exhausted.

Champagne Cocktails

lump sugar
bitters
orange rind
lemon peel

Place 1 small lump sugar into each champagne glass. Add a dash of bitters, 1 small twist of orange rind, and 1 small twist of lemon peel. Fill the glasses with champagne that has been iced.

These were everyone's favorite.

Pâté de Foie Gras
in Cream Cheese Balls

5 ounces of *Foie Gras*, ground into pâté
3 ounce package of cream cheese, softened
1 tablespoon Beau Monde seasoning
¼ cup chives, cleaned and snipped
3 tablespoons parsley, finely chopped

9 tablespoons of walnuts or pecans, chopped very finely

In a bowl blend *foie gras* pâté with cream cheese. Add Beau Monde seasoning, and blend. Using a wooden spoon, add chives and parsley. Mix well. Cover this mixture and refrigerate for at least 1 ½ hours. Roll the *foie gras*/cream cheese mixture into 1 inch balls, and then roll the balls into the chopped walnut or pecan mixture, making sure they are evenly coated.

They looked pretty, but very few tried them.

Quiche Tartlets

Pastry dough

1 ½ cups flour, sifted
1 teaspoon salt
½ cup shortening, softened
3 tablespoons ice water

1 egg yolk, beaten

2 tablespoons ice water

Filling

¾ cup sliced stuffed green olives
8 ounces of Swiss cheese, grated

2 eggs, beaten
1 cup cream
½ teaspoon salt
¼ teaspoon pepper
¼ teaspoon cayenne pepper
¼ teaspoon nutmeg

Sift the flour and salt into a bowl. Cut one-half of the softened shortening into the flour mixture with a pastry blender, then add the rest of the softened shortening and mix until the mixture is the size of very small olives. Sprinkle the ice water, 1 tablespoon at a time over the flour mixture, and blend. Add the ice water until the mixture holds together. Press the mixture into a ball, and with a rolling pin, roll out the dough mixture until it is ⅛ inch thick. Using a round dough or cookie cutter, cut the rolled out dough mixture into 2 ½ inch rounds. Fit the rounds into lightly greased muffin-pan cups.

Combine the beaten egg yolk and 2 tablespoons of water. With a pastry brush, brush this mixture over the inside of the shells.

Spoon chopped olives into each muffin-pan cup. Sprinkle 1 tablespoon of grated Swiss cheese into each muffin-pan cup.

Combine the beaten eggs, cream, salt, pepper, cayenne pepper and nutmeg, and beat. Pour 1 tablespoon of this mixture over the Swiss cheese and bake at 425° for eight minutes. Reduce the oven heat to 350° and bake for 5-7 minutes, or until the filling puffs up. Serve hot. This recipe makes 24 tartlets.

These tartlets can also be made using bacon, spinach or onion as the main ingredient. Mrs. E.O. Bittleduke chose olives because she thought the bacon was too unhealthy, she doesn't care for spinach, and Mrs. Grant Goldman-Hues has been known to break out in hives from onions.

Oyster *Bisque* Soup

14 tablespoons butter
1 cup flour
10 cups milk

1 cup yellow onions, diced
1 cup celery, chopped finely
2 tablespoons butter

4 cups of oysters, diced in juice
½ teaspoon garlic powder
½ teaspoon white pepper
1 cup sherry

In a saucepan, melt 14 tablespoons of butter. Slowly sift in 1 cup of flour. Using a whisk, stir continually over low heat for 2-3 minutes. Gradually add 10 cups of milk to the butter and flour mixture, stirring until the mixture has thickened.

In a separate pan, sauté chopped celery and onions in 2 tablespoons of butter until the vegetables are tender. Add 4 cups of diced oysters with juice and simmer the mixture until the edges of the oysters curl. This will take approximately 5 minutes. Add ½ teaspoon garlic powder, and ½ teaspoon white pepper to the oyster mixture. Combine the oyster mixture with the thickened milk mixture. Simmer for about 10 minutes. Add 1 cup of sherry and serve.

Maribelle Biche asked for the recipe.

Tarragon Carrots

3 teaspoons salt
2 dozen small carrots, cleaned and sliced thin

12 tablespoons butter, melted
3 tablespoons tarragon, chopped
5 teaspoons white wine vinegar
1 teaspoon honey

Boil the carrots in salt water until they are soft but not mushy. Drain well. Combine the melted butter, tarragon, white wine vinegar and honey. Pour over hot carrots. Stir and serve.

Bunny Baxley asked if anyone knew of a drink recipe that used tarragon. She said she liked the 'kick' in the spice.

Chicken *Croquettes*

⅔ cup butter
⅓ cup flour
1 quart cream
1 teaspoon salt
1 teaspoon pepper
2 teaspoons fresh parsley, finely chopped
2 teaspoons lemon juice
6 cups cooked chicken, cut finely

2 eggs, beaten
bread crumbs
cooking oil

In a saucepan, melt butter and slowly add the flour. Stir constantly until the mixture is thick and smooth. Add salt, pepper, parsley, and lemon juice to butter/flour mixture. Add cooked chicken. Spread the mixture on a platter and refrigerate until cold. Remove the mixture from the refrigerator and shape into balls. Dip the balls into the beaten eggs, then dip them into the bread crumbs. Roll them into oval shapes and deep fry the *croquettes* in hot oil until browned, or about 5 minutes. This recipe makes twelve *croquettes*.

Clove Cake

1 cup butter
2 cups sugar
5 eggs

3 cups flour, sifted
½ teaspoon cloves
½ teaspoon cinnamon
½ teaspoon allspice

1 teaspoon baking soda
½ cup molasses

butter for brushing

Cream butter and sugar. Beat eggs and add to the butter and sugar mixture. Combine the sifted flour with the cloves, cinnamon and allspice. Add baking soda to the molasses. Alternate adding the flour/spice mixture and the molasses/baking soda mixture to the butter/sugar/egg mixture. Pour into a greased tube pan. Bake at 350° for 45-55 minutes, or until the cake pulls away from the pan. While it is hot, brush the top of the cake with butter. Cool the cake before you remove it from the pan. To make a nice presentation, put a tablespoon of whipped cream on each serving.

Mrs. Michael Stellar raved on and on about this cake, and how it was so moist and tasty. Nobody else said anything about it, except Mrs. Samuel Squire who said she heard that it was one of Teddy Roosevelt's favorites.

Katrina Canfield's
Hawaiian Pool Party

Starters

Blue Hawaiian
Mai Tais
Bowls of Macadamia Nuts

Buffet

Display of Tropical Fruits
Pineapple-Cranberry Relish
Cooked Rice
Terriyaki Beef Skewers
Hawaiian Chicken
Broiled Veal Chops á la Canfield

Desserts

Baked Bananas
Pineapple Upside Down Cake

KATRINA CANFIELD'S POOL PATIO PARTY EXTRAVAGANZA

Everyone on The Executives' Wives' Cookbook Committee showed up for Katrina Canfield's summer pool and patio party extravaganza. It wasn't because Katrina Canfield was a well-liked, popular lady who made her guests feel like they were truly welcome. No, it was because most of the ladies on The Executives' Wives' Cookbook Committee knew, but would never acknowledge it, that Katrina had an innate ability to forecast future trends in fashion, food and fine things. So, of course, they came to see what was new.

They knew when they came to her party Katrina Canfield would be wearing the latest and most *avant-guard* fashions, and be sporting the most up-to-date hair design in both color and style. They knew they would be served the trendiest, nouvelle cuisine. They knew her contemporary home, her massive modern art collection, her taste in music and her marble pool would turn even a humble person green with envy. Above all, they all knew, without a doubt, that Katrina Canfield was truly 'cafe society,' which they longed to imitate, but didn't know how to do it without being labeled a 'copy-cat' by the other ladies.

Katrina Canfield worked hard to nonchalantly perfect and hone her blasé attitude and intimidating ways when The Executives' Wives' Cookbook Committee came for her party. As she once said to her husband, Blake, "It's how I am, who I am and you know I work hard to portray this image."

She realized that some of the ladies, like Mrs. Michael Stellar, Mrs. Jonathan Hurlinger, Mrs. Grant Goldman-Hues and Mrs. E.O. Bitleduke, really weren't as jealous and envious of her life-style as she had secretly hoped they would be. It was an irritant that she wanted to change, and it gnawed on her. Mrs. Elmer Steele and Maribelle Biche just plain irritated her. She once told her husband, "Why, nobody in their right mind should expect me to put up with Mrs. Elmer Steele, that bloated cow. She should have been 'milked for all she was worth' and 'put out to pasture long ago.' All she does is graze, anyway. Likewise, no one needs to think I would ever force-feed recipes to Biche the Beggar. I would just as soon go hungry as to do that."

She didn't have much time, or feel threatened or sorry for people like Martha Payne whom she thought was pathetically and hopelessly beyond help, or people like Mrs. Molly McCurdle whom she described as one who could never be a palatable person unless she 'puked out all her pinkness.' She basically ignored them. No matter how hard she tried, she couldn't ignore Doris Dupré, who she referred to as that deep, dark devil who needs to have her pitchfork exposed and turned around so she can shovel all the manure she had created, or her ex-best friend, Mrs. Christina Pebbleworth-Stafford, who became her #1 competitor, nemesis and one-up-man-ship threat. The bright side for Katrina was that Bunny Baxley, Beebe Hall, Mrs. Stanley Bigsbee and Mrs. Charles Chatterton loved her style, loved her flair and didn't have any problems feeding Katrina Canfield's ego, as long as she fed them their cocktails in a timely fashion.

Katrina Canfield, with her boundless energy and brilliant organizational skills, had her party planned in no time at all, even though the coordination of the massive amount of work that went into this undertaking would have overwhelmed most of the ladies on The Executives' Wives' Cookbook Committee. She hired and counted on numerous people to help in the washing of her glass house, the polishing of her marble pool and inlaid tile deck, the mowing of her expansive grounds, the wiring of all the outdoor lights and, of course, preparation of the food and the setting up of the elaborate Hawaiian buffet and bar. The day of the party, The Lawnboy came early because he knew his 'to do' list would include some more 'touch-up' trimming, 'touch-up' deck hosing, 'touch-up' glass polishing, 'touch-up' pool cleaning and anything that he saw that was a mandatory 'must-do.' In addition, she had hired him to be the bartender for the evening. All the ladies loved him, and she knew he would take care of their needs.

Katrina Canfield's party was scheduled to start at 6:00 p.m. on a hot, August evening. It was to start later than most parties because, as she said to Blake, "I want them in and out of here as fast as possible." She knew that most of them would be late and they were. Katrina Canfield had no sooner jumped into her new mini-skirt, the latest style that not even Mrs. Christina Pebbleworth-Stafford would own, when the Squires, looking like flags in drag, arrived. She stared at them and did everything in her power to make them feel uncomfortable. Thankfully for the Squires and for her, the Bittledukes, Hurlingers, Stellars and the Goldman-Hues all arrived a few minutes later. The ladies all looked lovely in their beautiful silk and linen and bolero summer sun dresses complete with matching sandals and tasteful handbags. The rest of The Executives' Wives' Cookbook Committee all arrived by 6:30 or shortly thereafter. When she saw others on the committee emerge from their cars, she pulled her husband aside and said, "Where do these people come from? They make the Squires look normal. Just because we're serving Hawaiian food, doesn't mean it's Halloween." But, it was a parade like nothing else she had ever seen come into their home. She expected better.

Mrs.Charles Chatterton and Mrs. Stanley Bigsbee came dressed in Alfred Shaheen silk, hand-printed sun dresses. They were beautiful, but just the idea of someone wearing a Hawaiian print dress was, well, just plain tacky to Katrina Canfield. What made it worse was seeing their husbands in Hawaiian shirts. They looked like they just got off the boat with Don Ho. She was horrified when she saw Mrs. Elmer Steele, bigger than life, in a red-flowered *mu mu,* and Mr. Elmer Steele, dressed like Ernest Hemingway, who was about to go on a hunt. "Why do I have to be with these people?" she lamented to herself. The parade got worse. "Look at the lollipops," she said to herself when she saw Mrs. Molly McCurdle arriving in a strapless, pink sun dress that was belted at the waist, connected to a full skirt over yards and yards of tulle can-cans. She was holding hands with her pink-shirted husband. She said to her husband, "Here comes the Pepto people – what a bismal, I mean dismal sight."

When Bunny Baxley arrived, and she saw she had an *"Itsy Bitsy, Teenie Weenie, Yellow Polk-a-dot Bikini"* on under her grass skirt, and see-through gauze, off the shoulder blouse, she shuddered and thought to herself, "I hope she doesn't think that this pool party is for swimming." It got worse. Beebe Hall, in a grass skirt and a coconut bra-top, was carrying a hula hoop. She had all she could take of this aloha attire and felt a 'fight or flight' sensation coming on when in walked Doris Dupré with an outfit made of hemp. Actually, Katrina Canfield thought the outfit was rather stylish, but the fact that she couldn't stand Doris Dupré, and she came in something maybe even Katrina Canfield hadn't realized was another new style, set her off. She couldn't resist saying to Doris Dupré, "Does that fiber grow in your yard or do the bunnies eat it all up?" She was relieved that Martha Payne had canceled at the last minute, and more relieved when Mrs. Christina Pebbleworth-Stafford, who always wanted to be the last one to arrive so as to make a grand entrance, came in wearing white, Capri-styled pants, topped off with everything else that Jackie Kennedy had made fashionable, including the style of her sunglasses. Katrina wasn't threatened by Christina's style. It was nothing new, the masses were on to it and Katrina made up her mind she was going to let her know it. She said, "Where's the pillbox?" Mrs. Christina Pebbleworth-Stafford, not missing a beat and obviously annoyed that Katrina Canfield's mini-skirt was a new fashion she wasn't on to yet, opened her purse, took out her pill box, opened it and said, "I have something in here that you might like. It makes a person bearable." The fight had started and so had the cocktails.

The Lawnboy was so busy filling glasses he didn't have time to realize what was taking place. Mr. Blake Canfield's job was to greet the guests by the pool and hand everyone a *lei.* After the guests had received their *leis* and started drinking, all sorts of inappropriate chatter was heard.

Bunny started it. Because she had hurried over to the bar before Mr. Blake Canfield could greet her and give her a *lei,* it took a while before she realized that she was the only one without one. She yelled, "I want a *lei.* Where do I get one?" Of course, the men started to laugh. Mrs. Elmer Steele didn't think it was funny. She ignored them and before most of them had downed their third drinks, she had already been up at the buffet table twice. Upon seeing this, Mrs. Stanley Bigsbee whispered to Mrs. Charles Chatterton, "All she needs is a parrot on her shoulder to complete the outfit, and for someone to keep her in line by yelling out, 'one at a time please,' every time she jumps on the scale." The Squires didn't laugh either. Mr. Samuel Squire was so busy giving, to anyone within earshot, a history lesson on Hawaii, its recent statehood and the motto of Hawaii, that being 'the life of the land is perpetuated in righteousness', that he wasn't paying attention to anything but himself. But, as was further witnessed at this party, there wasn't a whole lot of righteousness going on. Mrs. Christina Pebbleworth-Stafford, who had planned to get even with Mrs. Elmer Steele, went over to Mr. Elmer Steele, and right in front of Mrs. Elmer Steele said, "I need a new *lei*." Mrs. Steele was furious. Christina Pebbleworth-Stafford left the area, but she had made her point.

All of a sudden, Doris Dupré, who came out of nowhere, had taken off her hemp dress and stripped down to a skimpy swimming suit. She went to the diving board, and cannon-balled off the board, getting most of The Executives' Wives' Cookbook Committee a little wet. Katrina Canfield, madder than a wet hen, had just gone over to the side of the pool to confront Doris Dupré, when, all of a sudden, Beebe Hall and Bunny Baxley, now, at this point stripped down to their bikinis, followed suit and cannon-balled off the diving board. [44] In a split second any sort of rational order and decency came to an abrupt halt.

Mr. Elmer Steele, stripped down to his skivvies, tried to dive into the pool, but belly-flopped. Other men followed suit, and it was mayhem.

When Mrs. Stanley Bigsbee, and Mrs. Charles Chatterton, who had been on the same synchronized swimming team in their youth, jumped in fully clothed, nobody, at this point, paid any attention to them. They should have. Thank goodness The Lawnboy, who was trying to control the pandemonium, saw what was unfolding. It was obvious that Mrs. Charles Chatterton had immediately gone into one of her narcoleptic phases as soon as she hit the cold water. What everyone (including Mrs. Bigsbee) didn't see, was that her friend, Mrs. Charles Chatterton, sank to the bottom. The Lawnboy jumped in, fully clothed and pulled her up and

over to the side of the pool. He threw her over his shoulder and onto the deck. Realizing she wasn't breathing, he immediately started mouth-to-mouth resuscitation.

At this point, Mr. Blake Canfield yelled for everyone to get out of the pool immediately, or he would have to call the police. His voice was so loud and convincing that everyone jumped out of the pool, some slower than others depending on inebriation or age. Upon hearing this Dr. E. O. Bittleduke, who was in his own world, yelled, "Olly, Olly, Oxen Free." Mrs. E.O. Bittleduke looked at him sternly, put her finger over her lips to tell him to be quiet and was thankful there was a lot of commotion going on so no one would have heard him.

Everyone gathered around The Lawnboy and Mrs. Charles Chatterton. Bunny Baxley, who was jumping up and down and acting as inappropriately as always, said, "Oh, look at him. He's so handsome and strong. I wish I were Mrs. Chatterton right now." Nobody responded to Bunny Baxley, but everyone was relieved when Mrs. Charles Chatterton opened her eyes and in a weak voice said, "Where's my Old Golds?" Mrs. Stanley Bigsbee, her best friend, ran to get them and, came back with a lit cigarette. She handed it to her and said, "Wait, before you take a drag, I need to put some lipstick on you. Yours must not be water-proof."
The evening ended rather abruptly. Katrina Canfield vowed, never again — and especially when The Lawnboy, who was cleaning up, came over to her and said, "I found a bunch of lucky rabbits' feet at the bottom of the pool. How do you suppose they got there?" She smiled at The Lawnboy, thanked him profusely for all he had done and secretly planned her revenge.

And it was, indeed, a 'bigger splash.' One could say a splash bigger than anyone could imagine, and the ring and waves from the repercussions of the 'bigger splash' pooled and circled out for years; it left no one on The Executives' Wives' Cookbook Committee untouched, except Martha Payne, who wasn't there, and that was a good thing. She lived in a world where the waves come crashing.

[44] *Because neither of these ladies had any 'meat on their bones,' nobody got wet.*

Blue Hawaiian

1 ounce light rum or vodka
1 ounce blue *Curacao*
1 ounce coconut cream
3 ounces pineapple juice
lime or pineapple wedges

In a blender, blend the rum or vodka, *Curaco*, coconut cream and pineapple juice. Fill a cocktail glass or goblet 3/4 full of crushed ice. Add the drink. Garnish with a wedge of lime or pineapple.

This is the drink that got Mr. Elmer Steele in big trouble.

Mai Tais

1 ounce light rum
1 ounce dark rum
½ ounce crème de almond
1 ounce orange *Curacao*
2 ounces of orange or pineapple juice

Pour the ingredients into a Tom Collins glass and add shaved ice. Stir and serve with garnishes of pineapple wedges or Maraschino cherries.

This is the drink that just about put Mrs. Charles Chatterton 'under for good.'

Pineapple – Cranberry Relish

2 cans crushed pineapple (20 ounces)
2 large navel oranges, unpeeled
2 packages fresh cranberries (12 ounce)
1 ½ teaspoons lemon juice
2 cups sugar
2 packages frozen strawberries, (16 ounces each) thawed and drained

Drain syrup from pineapple. In a food processor or blender, chop oranges and cranberries until they are cut into coarse pieces. Pour into a bowl. Add the pineapple, lemon juice, sugar and strawberries. Cover with plastic wrap, and refrigerate overnight. Leave the top of the pineapple intact and cut it in half. Scoop out the inside. Mound the pineapple-cranberry relish in the 'pineapple boat'.

Mrs. Christina Pebble-worth Stafford said to her husband, "I wonder if she made relish as some kind of joke? I don't think it's very funny, and it's certainly not sophisticated."

Teriyaki Beef Skewers

2 pounds sirloin of beef
2 cans chunk pineapple (20 ounce cans)
¼ cup brown sugar
1 cup sherry
½ cup soy sauce
2 cloves garlic, chopped finely
2 teaspoons fresh ginger root, chopped

Cut the sirloin into 1-inch cubes. Mix the brown sugar, sherry, soy sauce, garlic and ginger root. Pour this mixture over the cubed sirloin and marinate for approximately 6 hours. Alternate putting cubes of meat and pineapple chunks on skewers. Grill on a charcoal grill.

Mrs. Elmer Steele's hands and feet swelled up from the soy sauce.

Hawaiian Style Chicken

8 chickens, quartered
1 cup pineapple juice concentrate
1 cup soy sauce
1 cup ketchup
2 ½ cups white wine
2 tablespoons ginger
2 pineapples, chunked

Wash and quarter the chickens. In a bowl combine the pineapple juice, soy sauce, ketchup, white wine and ginger. Pour the mixture over the chicken. Cover, refrigerate and marinate for 4 hours. Baste and turn the chicken while grilling. Place the grilled chicken on a large platter and surround it with the pineapple chunks.

Maribelle Biche asked for this recipe, but didn't get it.

Grilled Veal Chops á la Canfield

12 veal chops, 1-1 ½" thick
olive oil
salt
black pepper, freshly cracked

9 tablespoons unsalted butter
6 pounds, shiitake mushrooms, thinly sliced
1 cup dry sherry

Rub the veal chops with olive oil, and season with salt and pepper. Grill the veal chops for approximately 10 minutes on each side. Keep warm.

In a separate pan, melt the butter, and add the shiitake mushrooms. Sauté for approximately 10 minutes. Add the dry sherry and continue cooking for a couple of minutes.

When serving, pour the mushroom sauce over the veal chops.

This was Katrina Canfield's own creation. Mrs. Christina Pebbleworth-Stafford knew it and was jealous. She made a point not to compliment her on any of her recipes.

Baked Bananas

12 bananas, peeled and halved lengthwise
½ cup butter
⅔ cup brown sugar
½ teaspoon ground cloves
3 tablespoons orange juice
6 tablespoons rum
⅔ cup shredded coconut
1 cup chopped Macadamia nuts

In a small bowl, combine cream, the butter and sugar. Stir in cloves, orange juice and rum, and mix until smooth. Place the bananas in a 9" x 12" baking dish. Pour the mixture evenly over the bananas. Sprinkle with coconut and Macadamia nuts. Bake at 375° for approximately 10 minutes, or until the bananas are bubbly.

Bunny Baxley thought these were cute, even though she didn't try them. Beebe Hall took out her lighter, added a little Ever Clear that was in a small bottle in her purse, and tried to ignite it. It didn't work very well.

Pineapple Upside Down Cake

¼ cup butter
½ cup brown sugar
1 can whole pineapple slices
1 jar maraschino cherries

1 cup cake flour, sifted
1 teaspoon baking powder
½ teaspoon salt
¼ cup butter
½ cup milk
1 egg
½ teaspoon almond extract
½ teaspoon vanilla extract

1 pint whipping cream
½ cup sugar
1 ½ teaspoons vanilla

Put butter in an 8 inch pan and melt it in the oven. Take the pan out of the oven and sprinkle the brown sugar over the butter. Place individual pineapple slices over the brown sugar/butter mixture and put a Maraschino cherry in the center of each pineapple slice.

In a bowl, sift the cake flour, baking powder and salt. Add the butter, milk, egg, almond and vanilla extracts. Beat for a couple of minutes and pour the batter over the pineapple slices in the 8 inch pan. Put the cake back in the oven and bake.

Pour the whipping cream into a bowl, add the sugar and vanilla and beat into stiff peaks. Serve with whipped cream, topped with a Maraschino cherry on each piece.

This was such an old-fashioned dessert that most of the ladies were surprised that Katrina served it. They all know she does what she wants and tries to keep the other ladies in the dark.

119

Mrs. Martha Payne's Summer Luncheon

BEVERAGES

Iced Tea & Coffee

HORS D'OEUVRES

Assorted Cheese Tray with Crackers

Steak Tartare

SOUP

Gazpacho

MAIN COURSE

Crabmeat Remoulade

DESSERT

Vanilla Ice Cream

Lime Sherbet

MARTHA PAYNE'S SUMMER LUNCHEON

Due to her unfortunate, ill health, the only time Martha Payne feels up to entertaining is in the summer. She hosted a summer luncheon for the ladies of The Executives' Wives' Cookbook Committee at a time when she knew several of them would be on holiday. Of course, the poor dear didn't do this to be mean or spiteful, but large crowds just made her nervous and she knew from firsthand experience that hosting a party at her home could send her off to bed for weeks. Just thinking about it became a bitter pill to swallow.

Another phobia that Martha Payne was trying to conquer was her fear of fire and ice. Consequently, her ability to prepare and serve food was limited to cold dishes. However, with encouragement from her loving husband, Dr. Theodore Payne III, and the patience The Executives' Wives' Cookbook Committee has tried to bestow upon her, Martha musters up the courage to host at least one luncheon a year, [45] and she knows this luncheon is a 'must do'.

The week before the luncheon, Martha took ill but managed to pull herself together, thanks to the fact that the new medicine her husband prescribed for her kicked into high gear.

There were seven guests who made it to her luncheon. They were Mrs. Michael Stellar, Mrs. Stanley Bigsbee, Mrs. Jonathan Hurlinger, Mrs. Charles Chatterton, Mrs. Molly McCurdle, Bunny Baxley and Beebe Hall.

She was relieved that Doris Dupré, Mrs. Christina Pebbleworth-Stafford, Maribelle Biche and Mrs. Elmer Steele were on holiday. Those four ladies made her nervous. She knew Katrina Canfield wouldn't be coming because she always has had an excuse in the past. She figured it would be no different this year. She was right. Mrs. Samuel Squire couldn't come because she and her husband were attending the "National Descendants of George Washington Family Reunion." [46] Mrs. E.O. Bittleduke couldn't make it because 'The Doctor' was having a rough week and Mrs. Grant Goldman-Hues canceled at the last minute because she had either misplaced or someone had stolen one of her five carat diamond earrings.

The day that Martha Payne hosted her summer luncheon, Beebe Hall and Bunny Baxley made a day of it. They knew Martha didn't serve alcohol because cocktails are made with either fire or ice. They started their day at the Baxley's home for Bloody Marys, then went to the Hall's home to have a flaming drink and ended up making a quick trip to the country club lounge for a refresher before they arrived at Martha Payne's home. Needless to say, they were late,

---

[45] Only twice has she had to cancel it in the last seven years.

[46] This reunion is by invitation only; not just anyone can show up.

and inappropriately dressed. Martha didn't mind because they were always cordial, relaxed and made the day entertaining with their slurred words and unsteady walks. Both Bunny Baxley and Beebe Hall have been patients of Martha's husband. They know he is well-respected and doesn't make light of important issues.

Because they both have some peculiar issues to battle, Martha Payne felt a special bond with Mrs. Molly McCurdle. It helps her immensely to know she's not the only one with deep-seated problems.

It's easy for her to have Mrs. Jonathan Hurlinger and Mrs. Michael Stellar at her home. They are both genuinely gracious and complimentary, and speak in such a gentle way.

As usual, Mrs. Stanley Bigsbee and Mrs. Charles Chatterton showed up together. They are loyal to their friends on The Executives' Wives' Cookbook Committee and they rarely miss a luncheon.

Nothing out of the ordinary happened at Martha Payne's luncheon. After it was over, her husband complimented her on her ability to stay calm. She was relieved that her turn to serve her recipes for The Executives' Wives' Cookbook was over and done.

Cheese Tray

Martha Payne always served a cheese tray that was over flowing with a variety of imported cheeses such as Gouda, Camembert, Brie, Cheddar and Havarti and was tastefully decorated with fresh green parsley. The cheese was always bordered by small crackers, Melba toast and rye-bread wedges.

Bunny Baxley really didn't care for food, but she liked to play with it. When Martha Payne wasn't looking, she took a small piece of cheddar cheese, playfully put it in front of her teeth, looked at Beebe Hall, smiled and said, "Say cheese!"

Steak *Tartare*

2 teaspoons Dijon mustard
2 tablespoons lemon juice
1 small onion, finely chopped
8 anchovy fillets, finely chopped
1 teaspoon salt
1 teaspoon pepper
2 tablespoons heavy cream
5 tablespoons cognac
2 pounds top sirloin, freshly ground
parsley, chopped

Mix the mustard with the lemon juice. Add the onion and anchovy fillets. Sprinkle in the salt and pepper before adding the cream and cognac. Using two forks, carefully add the freshly ground top sirloin to the blended mixture. Shape the Steak *Tartare* into small meatball-sized balls and roll them in chopped parsley. Serve with toothpicks.

Mrs. Stanley Bigsbee and Mrs. Charles Chatterton loved their Steak Tartare and went back for seconds. Bunny Baxley tried it after they told her it had cognac in it. She asked for the recipe because she thought it would be healthy food for her poodle, Fifi.

Gazpacho Soup

6 ripe tomatoes, quartered
1 large cucumber, diced
1 onion, finely minced
2 scallions, finely chopped
1 clove garlic, finely chopped
½ large red pepper, chopped and seeded
½ large green pepper, chopped and seeded
½ cup parsley, finely chopped
4 tablespoons red wine vinegar
⅓ cup olive oil
2 cups of tomato juice
1 ½ teaspoon salt
1 teaspoon pepper

Place the above ingredients in a blender. Don't puree, but stop blending while there are still fairly large chunks of vegetables visible. Cover and refrigerate. Serve chilled. Decorate each soup bowl with a dollop of sour cream for an artistic presentation.

Mrs. Stanley Bigsbee wanted to find a lipstick shade that was the color of the soup. Beebe Hall and Bunny Baxley didn't even try the soup.

Crabmeat *Remoulade*

6 cups of fresh crab meat
salad greens

Remoulade sauce
2 cups of mayonnaise
½ cup parsley, chopped
½ cup onion, chopped
1 clove garlic, finely chopped
1 teaspoon Beau Monde seasoning
2 teaspoons Dijon mustard

3 hard-boiled eggs, finely chopped
capers
pansies

Shred the crab meat and chill. Arrange the crab meat on a colorful variety of fresh, salad greens. To make the *remoulade* sauce, combine the mayonnaise, parsley, onion, garlic, Beau Monde seasoning and Dijon mustard in a bowl and stir. Cover the crab meat with the *remoulade* sauce. Garnish with chopped eggs, capers and pretty, edible pansies.

Both Mrs. Michael Stellar and Mrs. Jonathan Hurlinger commented on how delicious it tasted and what a pretty touch the pansies added. They were always so generous with compliments, even though both of them left half of their food on their plates.

Vanilla Ice Cream

6 egg whites
1 ½ cups of sugar
6 egg yolks
¼ cup whole milk
2 cups whipping cream
2 ¼ teaspoons pure vanilla extract

Beat the egg whites until they form stiff peaks. Gradually add the sugar. In a separate bowl, beat the egg yolks until they are creamy. Add the milk and combine it with the egg white/sugar meringue. In another bowl beat the whipping cream until it forms soft peaks. Add the vanilla. Gently fold and combine both mixtures. Freeze until the ice cream has set.

Martha Payne decided to conquer her fear of ice. She swallowed 3 doses of medicine, and ended up in the bathroom for 2 hours while Dr. Payne took over and made the ice cream and it was a hit.

Lime Sherbet

Martha Payne was going to try to make lime sherbet from scratch. When she realized that homemade sherbet calls for boiling syrup, she purchased it instead.

MRS. CHRISTINA PEBBLEWORTH STAFFORD'S

French Dinner

APERTIF
Kir
Les Croquemitaines
Amuse-Guele au Roquefort

PAIN
Pain de Campagne

SOUPE
Vichyssoise

ENTRÉE
Beujalais
Haricots Verts á la Crème
Pomme de Tèrre
Bouef á la Bourguignonne

FROMAGE
Fromage de Chévre
Brie
Camembert

DÉSERT
Mousse au Chocolat

AFTER DINNER
Cognac and Cigars for Men in the Library
Coffee and Dark Chocolates for Women in the Parlor

MRS. CHRISTINA PEBBLEWORTH-STAFFORD'S FRENCH DINNER, SI VOUS PLAIT

Mrs. Christina Pebbleworth-Stafford knew her family's *fait accomplis* were legendary and, with a passion, she continually pursued her goal to make sure no acquaintance of either her or her husband's came close to rival the lofty self-imposed standards they set for themselves.

The Executives' Wives' Cookbook Committee knew that when they arrived at the Pebbleworth-Stafford home for her recipe-tasting party they would not only be treated to the utmost in cuisine and conversation, but that they also would be subject to cold shoulder treatments from this café society, socially sophisticated, *savior faire* couple who, rumor has it, believed that the ladies of The Executive Wives' Cookbook Committee were 'dreadfully dull'.

Knowing what she would demand of herself to host The Executives' Wives' Cookbook Committee for her recipe-tasting party, it didn't surprise anyone on the cookbook committee that she requested to be one of the last ones to host.

Mrs. Christina Pebbleworth-Stafford and her husband were undergoing a massive renovation of both their stately home and the grounds. It not only took its toll on them, but also the workers. All the hiring and firing she did consumed her time. It was the one thing she had difficulty managing. But, manage she did, and had everything in order when the day of her party finally arrived.

As the guests arrived and the valets parked their cars, the Pebbleworth-Staffords formally greeted each and every one of them. Dressed in Chanel, Christina Pebbleworth-Stafford invited them into her home. When Doris Dupré, looked at the grounds and saw that the Pebbleworth-Stafford *parterres* were larger and better groomed than hers, she could hardly stand to shake hands. When she entered the house, she had all she could do to silence her inner rage and start to plan how she was going to get even.

After the Baxleys and Halls had shaken hands with the Pebbleworth-Staffords and they were out of range of earshot from them, Beebe Hall whispered to Bunny Baxley, "Oh Lord, I wonder if there is a hall of mirrors in here. I need to touch up my lipstick." Bunny Baxley laughed, gestured in the direction to the right of her and said to her friend, Beebe Hall, "Over here, Madame. Welcome to the Versailles."

The Biches and the Steeles came together. When Maribelle Biche saw the 'excess', she whispered to Mrs. Elmer Steele, "You know what happened to Marie Antoinette when she got this carried away. I came for the food, not for an oh, look at me and my beautiful home, and my pretty clothes, and my slim figure, and don't forget to get jealous of my perfect husband." Katrina Canfield gave Mrs. Christina Pebbleworth-Stafford an 'I'm forced to shake your hand and you know it's only a handshake', and walked right in like she owned the place. Martha Payne anticipated that she would be having strange feelings and pre-medicated herself up to the point where she seemed to be at ease.[47] The Squires, like usual, came dressed in red, white and blue. She made a point to say, "I see you have your French flag colors on. Thank you for honoring the spirit of the meal." She knew Mr. Samuel Squire would start in on an exposé right away, so before he could get a word out of his mouth she excused herself and went inside until she saw he was done giving her husband an earful on French and English history. When she returned, the parade was starting. Mrs. Molly McCurdle, dressed like Clara from the Nutcracker, curtsied after she shook her hand. After staring her down, Mrs. Christina Pebbleworth-Staffore had a hard time greeting her. When Mrs. Molly McCurdle and her husband had gone into the house, Mrs. Christina Pebbleworth-Stafford rolled her dark eyes and whispered to her husband, "She needs to be committed, and the sooner the better."

---

[47] *It bothered Mrs. Christina Pebbleworth-Stafford that Martha Payne was totally at ease. She was hoping she hadn't lost her touch of intimidating those who were easy targets.*

The Bittledukes, Stellars, Goldman-Hues and Hurlingers came together. After they shook hands with the Pebbleworth-Staffords and entered the house, Mr. David Pebbleworth-Stafford gently poked his wife and said, "Look at them, they're gawking and wandering around like a group of people on a first-time bus tour of the Louvre. We should be selling posters of the Mona Lisa to help pay for this renovation."

The Chattertons and Bigsbees were the last to arrive. Each of them came carrying a bottle of Sauvignon Cabernet. She quickly looked at the bottles and knew immediately they really didn't have sophisticated palates when it came to French wine, but she thanked them politely. When they surveyed the house, Mrs. Charles Chatterton looked at her friend, Mrs. Stanley Bigsbee, and said, "Maybe we could play hide-and-seek in here. It's so large I think people would have a hard time finding us, and the truth is, that was exactly what happened."

After the guests were seated, Mr. David Pebbleworth-Stafford gave a toast and thanked everyone for coming. When he was finished, his wife stood up and toasted the ladies, only her toast had a *quid pro quo* in it with a strong message. Without batting an eyelash she said, "The return on our investment should be that we see children in distress that exhibit, even if it's crude, a rudimentary sense of sophistication. With that in mind, I was hoping our charity money would be used to fund traveling art exhibits, instead of library books. Also, I think it wise if we skip the puppies in distress. They can fend for themselves."

Bunny looked puzzled and said, "If that doesn't work, I can always do magic tricks with swizzle sticks for children in distress and puppies too. *Fifi* gets so excited when I perform my magic. She starts chasing her tail, gets dizzy and acts like she's drunk." [48] Beebe Hall thought Bunny Baxley's idea was brilliant and said, "I can show them how to safely light fireworks and give private pyrotechnics classes." Bunny Baxley got excited when she heard about Beebe Hall's ideas and her mind was like her drink, overflowing. She continued, "I know how to work a hula hoop from the head all the way down to the knees and up to the head

again." Mrs. Christina Pebbleworth-Stafford looked at Beebe Hall and Bunny Baxley, and for once, she was at a loss for words. She sat down and requested that the meal be brought in immediately. Out of the blue, Doris Dupré announced that she wasn't feeling well and left. Everyone thought it was odd, but everyone thought she was odd, too.

Shortly after they had started eating, Dr. E.O. Bittleduke excused himself and a couple of minutes later so did Mrs. Charles Chatterton. Fifteen minutes had gone by and neither of them had returned. Mrs. E.O. Bittleduke politely excused herself, and when after fifteen minutes she didn't return, Mrs. Christina Pebbleworth-Stafford excused herself, went into the kitchen and asked The Lawnboy to hunt for them. Mrs. Stanley Bigsbee excused herself and followed The Lawnboy, but couldn't keep up with him so she got lost.

It took only a few minutes for The Lawnboy to round up the lost guests. He found Dr. E.O. Bittleduke in the *parterres*. He was talking to a topiary thinking it was a patient. The Lawnboy heard him say, "I guarantee you, you will feel younger and look younger, and at your age you don't need those parts anyway." The Lawnboy, much to everyone's relief, steered Dr. E.O. Bittleduke back to the table. On his way in he saw Mrs. E.O. Bittleduke on the other end of the *parterres*, so he ran out to the garden, again, and guided her back to the table. Now, he only had two left to find. Based on previous experience, he knew it wouldn't be easy.

When he opened the door to the Pebbleworth-Stafford's enormous wine cellar, he saw Mrs. Charles Chatterton passed out on the floor with Mrs. Stanley Bigsbee trying to pour a drink down her throat. He heard Mrs. Stanley Bigsbee say, "Charlotte, just take a drink of this. It's sure to give you a jolt and wake you up." He went over to the ladies and lifted Mrs. Charles Chatterton into a sit-up position. He told Mrs. Stanley Bigsbee to wait while he ran to get help. In no time at all The Lawnboy and another staff member had carried both ladies out of the wine cellar and set them on a couch. The Lawnboy was relieved that they both seemed okay, but he was horrified when

[48] *Everyone knew she probably was drunk.*

126

he saw that Mrs. Charles Chatterton, in her stupor had broken a bottle of Chateau Savignon from the Chateau Mouton Rothschild's 1945 harvest. He knew it was one of the Pebbleworth-Stafford's prized bottles and he knew he had no choice but to tell them. They took the news better than he had expected. The Lawnboy heard her say to her husband, "I should have known better than to think this committee was good enough for me. I learned my lesson and it will never happen again."

When The Lawnboy was cleaning up, the phone rang and he answered it. He went into the front room where the Pebbleworth-Staffords were having a nightcap and announced, "Excuse me, but there was a lady on the phone who had a muffled voice. All she said was, "*Vini Vidi Vici*," and then she hung up. Mrs. Christina Pebbleworth-Stafford looked at her husband and said, "It must have been a wrong number."[49]

Kir

2 tablespoons *Crème de Cassis*
6 ounces dry white wine
twist of lemon peel

Pour the *Crème de Cassis* in a white wine glass, then add the dry white wine. Put a few ice cubes in the wine glass, and top with a twist of lemon peel.

Most of the men would have preferred a Manhattan over Kir, but a person doesn't always get exactly what he wants in life.

Les Croquemitaines

16 slices ham, boiled
8 slices *Gruyére* cheese, sliced thin

1 egg
1 teaspoon vegetable oil
2 teaspoons salt
2 teaspoons pepper

1 ½ cups flour
1 ½ cups breadcrumbs, dry

⅓ cup butter, melted

Cut ham into 2 inch squares. Cover each piece with a 2-inch square slice of *Gruyére* cheese. On top of the cheese place another piece of ham that has been cut into a 2 inch square.

In a bowl, beat the egg. Add the vegetable oil, salt and pepper and beat again.

Place the flour and dry bread crumbs on two separate plates. Roll the ham cheese squares into the flour, and then dip them in the egg mixture. Spoon the breadcrumbs onto the squares and pat the breadcrumbs into the ham/cheese squares. Place the squares on a buttered, baking sheet and drizzle melted butter over each square. Bake at 375° for approximately 5 minutes.

According to Mrs. Grant Goldman-Hues, these were more about taste than about looks.

Amuse-Gueule Au Roquefort

1 pound *Roquefort* cheese
¼ cup butter
¼ cup cream cheese
4 tablespoons chives, chopped
½ teaspoon salt
½ teaspoon pepper
¼ teaspoon cayenne pepper
1 dash of hot sauce
2 teaspoons cognac

In a bowl, crush and mix the Roquefort cheese, butter and cream cheese. Beat in the chives, salt, pepper, cayenne pepper, hot sauce and cognac. Roll into dainty ½ inch balls. Roll the balls into chopped walnuts or stale breadcrumbs. Chill. Serve on a platter edged in small, red grape bunches.

---

[49]*Mrs. Christina Pebbleworth-Stafford, mulled over the phone call for a few days, and then she forgot about it until a week later when her gardener announced that her parterre was overrun with rabbits. Instantly it hit her, she knew, without a doubt what Vini Vidi Vici was all about, and she planned her revenge.*

Vichyssoise

6 potatoes, peeled, chopped and quartered
6 leeks, chopped
2 teaspoons salt

3 cups whipping cream
1 bunch parsley, chopped

Bring the potatoes, leeks and salt to a boil. Reduce heat and simmer for approximately 30 minutes in a covered pan. When the vegetables are soft, put them, with the stock, into a blender and purée. Place in soup bowls and add whipping cream. Serve either hot or cold and garnish with chopped parsley.

Mrs. Christina Pebbleworth-Stafford would have preferred to serve French onion soup rather than Vichyssoise. She couldn't because Beebe Hall had already served it at her flaming flambé. As Mrs. Christina Pebbleworth-Stafford said to Mrs. Elmer Steele, "What a shame she was allowed to serve French onion soup. She made a 'fiery' mess out of it."

Pain de Campagne

2 packages dry yeast
1 teaspoon sugar
2 ½ cups warm water

6 cups flour
1 ½ teaspoons salt

1 egg white
1 tablespoon water

Dissolve the yeast and sugar in the warm water. Let stand until the yeast is dissolved and starts to bubble. Stir in the flour and salt. Let rise for about 45 minutes. Knead the bread on a floured board for approximately 8 to 10 minutes. Put the dough in a large bowl and cover. Let it rise for 2 ½ to 3 hours. Remove the dough from the bowl and punch down again. Divide the dough in half and roll into two 12 x 6 inch rectangles. Roll and shape the dough into two loaves. Place the bread dough on cookie sheets. Let rise for about 1¼ hours. Cut slashes in the top of the bread and bake at 400° for about 20 minutes. Remove from the oven and brush with egg white/water mixture. Return to oven and bake for approximately 15 more minutes.

Several of the guests saw Doris Dupré put a whole loaf of bread in her large handbag. She didn't even pretend to hide what she was doing. She was as Maribelle Biche said to Mrs. E.O. Bittleduke, "deer who wandered into the city limits in the middle of the day and grazed on everyone's garden like she owned it."

Haricots Verts á la Crème

6 pounds green beans, snipped and washed
2 teaspoons salt
2 teaspoons pepper
6 tablespoons unsalted butter
4 cups of heavy cream

In a pot of boiling water, blanch the beans until they are almost tender. Drain them. Add the salt, pepper and butter. Pour the cream over the beans and boil until tender.

When Bunny Baxley served herself string beans, she looked at Beebe Hall and said, "I feel like Popeye." Beebe Hall said, "No, Bunny, that was spinach, remember?" Bunny Baxley replied, "Oh yes, but they all look and taste the same to me."

Pomme de Tèrre

16 small potatoes
2 teaspoons salt

2 teaspoons salt
2 teaspoons pepper
½ cup butter melted
1 bunch parsley, snipped

Place the potatoes in salt water and bring to a boil. Turn down the heat and simmer for approximately 25 minutes, or until potatoes are tender but not mushy. Drain well. Salt and pepper the potatoes. In a bowl, toss the potatoes with melted butter and parsley.

Maribelle Biche thought the potatoes had too much butter on them. She had the nerve to announce it at the table so everyone could hear.

Bouef á la Bourguignonne

6 pounds chuck steak, boneless
8 pieces bacon, cut into small pieces
2 tablespoons brandy
4 onions, finely chopped
2 garlic cloves, finely chopped
4 tablespoons flour
3 cups red wine
1 cup beef broth

Bouquet Garni

6 sprigs parsley
2 bay leaves
1 teaspoon fresh thyme
1 teaspoon peppercorns

salt
pepper

4 tablespoons butter
2 pounds mushrooms, quartered
4 tablespoons parsley, freshly chopped

In a large skillet, fry the bacon. Remove the bacon from the pan, leaving the bacon grease in the pan. Remove the fat from the beef, and cut it into 1 inch cubes. Putting just a few pieces of beef in the pan at a time, sauté the beef in the bacon fat until it is lightly browned.

Place the beef and bacon in a large, 5 quart casserole and put it on a moderate heat. Add the brandy and flame it. Stir in the onions, garlic and flour. Next, add the wine and the beef broth. Bring this mixture to a simmering point.

Place the parsley, bay leaves, thyme and peppercorns in a cheesecloth bag. Place the bag in the casserole. Season everything with salt and pepper.

Bake at 350° for 1 ½ hours. Take the casserole out of the oven and cool. Chill it in the refrigerator overnight.

The next day place the casserole in the oven for 20 minutes at 350°.

In a fry pan melt the butter; add the mushrooms and sauté until lightly browned. Place the mushrooms into the casserole. Garnish with parsley and serve.

Mrs. Christina Pebbleworth-Stafford was a big fan of Julia Child, Jackie Kennedy and everyone else who knew French food, could appreciate French food and could cook French food. She worked hard with her chef to come up with her own Beef Bourguignonne recipe and thought it held its own with Julia's recipe.

Fromage

Fromage de Chévre
Brie
Camembert

Bunny announced to everyone that the only kind of cheese that she could eat was Velveeta. Nobody else would have dared to make that statement, especially at the Pebbleworth-Stafford home.

Mousse au Chocolat

8 ounces dark chocolate, chopped
4 tablespoons butter
1 tablespoon coffee liqueur

2 cups whipping cream
½ cup sugar
1 teaspoon vanilla extract

1 pint raspberries

In a double boiler, melt the chocolate and butter. Add the coffee liqueur and stir. Add the egg yolks one at a time, and stir until the mixture has thickened. Cool. Whip the cream, sugar and vanilla extract. Carefully fold it into the chocolate mixture. Serve the mousse in a wine or martini glass. Garnish with raspberries.

When Mr. Elmer Steele was eating his chocolate mousse, a raspberry seed lodged under his 'plates.' He excused himself and left the table. Mrs. Elmer Steele figured out what had happened and as soon as he left, she finished his chocolate mousse as well as her own.

Bunny's Hangover Brunch

Cocktail

BLOODY MARY

Main Course

SCOTCH EGGS
WHEAT TOAST WITH ASSORTED MARMALADES

After Breakfast Drink

BITTERS

Settling Drink

CHOCOLATE MILK

BUNNY'S HANGOVER BRUNCH

It has become a tradition for Bunny and Johnny Baxley to host Sunday afternoon hangover brunches. The idea for a Sunday hangover brunch was born a few years ago when one Sunday morning Bunny was suffering from a severe, hang-over headache. Johnny, made a brunch for her that, along with a few pills, *voila!* made her head-ache disappear. Bunny Baxley, the clever lady that she was known to be, decided right then and there that if it worked for her, it certainly would work for her dear friends. Besides, as she told her husband, Johnny, "We need to be more compassionate and help our friends who are suffering. We shouldn't just think of ourselves."

Bunny and Johnny always looked forward to Sunday afternoon brunch. Just having their close friends around, who were in the same situation as they were, always has helped them get through the day. [50] She has always told her friends, "If you wake up feeling like a Mac truck just drove over your head, come on over and we will fix you up and get you thinking clear before it's cocktail hour."

Most of their friends usually arrived at about 2:00 p.m. The party invariably lasted until about 5:00 p.m. If their friends were feeling pretty good and they decided to stay after 5:00 pm., Bunny would start mixing cocktails, and she would serve trays of saltine crackers and cans of mixed nuts so everyone could nibble! What a Bunny! Ta-da!

Bloody Mary

2 shots vodka
3 ounces tomato juice
1 teaspoon pepper
1 teaspoon salt
1 teaspoon lemon juice
2 splashes Worcestershire sauce
3 drops Tabasco sauce

Shake with ice and strain into old-fashioned glass over ice cubes. For garnishes, use a celery stick with leaves, 2 green olives or a wedge of lime. If you don't have any of these, put a dill pickle on the side and call it "Good enough."

Beebe Hall was helping Bunny Baxley compile her recipes one morning and they decided they had to 'sample' the drinks before they were put into the cookbook. Things got out of hand. Bunny Baxley was out of vodka, so they decided to substitute Southern Comfort for vodka. Neither of them cared much for tomato juice, so they decided to use charged water instead. When Bunny Baxley couldn't find a stalk of celery to use for garnish, she said to Beebe Hall, "Letsjusthopscotchit," which Beebe Hall knew meant, "Let's do without."

After those little problems were solved, Bunny Baxley instructed Beebe Hall to find the Worcestershire sauce. As Beebe Hall was looking for it, Bunny Baxley downed a shot of So Co. Beebe Hall, out of the corner of her eye, saw what she was doing and busted her. She poured herself a 'stiff one', raised her glass and said, "Here's to sneaky-peaky, best friends." Bunny Baxley, not one to be out-done, poured herself another drink, raised it and replied, "Birds of a feather drink together." Beebe Hall couldn't resist and responded, "Let's get back to Bloody Mary, quite contrary." By this time they were both laughing so hard that they decided to skip the whole 'bloody mess' and go shopping.

Scotch Eggs

12 hard boiled eggs
2 pounds pork sausage, ground
4 eggs, lightly beaten
bread crumbs, finely crushed

Peel the eggs and flour them lightly. Divide the sausage meat into 12 portions and flatten each section a bit. Flour your hands and wrap the sausage meat around the eggs. Next, flour the boiled eggs and dip them into the beaten eggs. Roll the boiled eggs into the bread crumbs. Deep fry the boiled eggs, blot

---

[50] *Even Doris Dupré has shown up a few times, let down her 'façade', and unfortunately helped herself to a few things.*

off the grease and chill. Put the boiled eggs on a platter surrounded with quarter slices of toast. Serve with a variety of marmalades.

There was not one lady who ever wanted to try a scotch egg. They did, however, sample a little toast to settle things down.

Bitters

2 pounds sour orange peel
4 teaspoons cardamom, ground
4 teaspoons anise seeds
4 teaspoons coriander
6 cups grain alcohol
boiling water
4 teaspoons caramel coloring, or 4 teaspoons coca cola

Bunny Baxley never made orange bitters because it was too time-consuming. Mrs. Elmer Steele had made it known that a recipe for orange bitters needed to be in the cookbook. Bunny Baxley decided to include the list of ingredients, but not the directions in the cookbook. She said to her friend, Beebe Hall, "Who in their right mind is going to make bitters? It would take someone with a mind like Albert Einstein to figure out how to make it."

She told her husband Johnny, "This ought to rattle Mrs. Steele's cage, and I'm going to rather enjoy watching her tizzy-fit."

Chocolate Milk

You may purchase ready-to-serve good quality, chocolate milk from your favorite dairy store or make it from scratch:

4 squares unsweetened chocolate
2 cups water
pinch of salt
6 tablespoons sugar

Heat the chocolate and water over low heat. Add salt and sugar; cook for 4 minutes, stirring constantly. Slowly add 6 cups milk and heat. Do not boil. Refrigerate immediately and beat with rotary mixer until smooth before serving in tall drinking glasses.

Bunny Baxley never made this because the milkman brought her chocolate milk and she had figured out a long time ago that it was easier to pour than to mix.

Bunny's Booze Bash

Cosmopolitan

Gin Swizzle

Gin Fizzzzzle Swizzzzzy a la Bunny

Tom Collins

Fuzzy Navel

Singapore Sling

Rusty Nail

Old Fashioned

Gin and Tonic

Sea Breeze

Piña Colada

Pink Lady

B-52

Brandy Alexander

Grasshopper

Hot Toddy

Manhattan

BUNNY'S BOOZE BASH FOR FIFI'S MEMORIAL PARTY

Two weeks before Bunny Baxley was to host The Executives' Wives' Cookbook Committee for a 'booze bash' as Johnny Baxley coined it, their beloved poodle, *Fifi*, expired. A tragedy of this proportion and magnitude had never happened to the Baxleys.

Bunny Baxley decided that it was only fitting to have a memorial for *Fifi* at the same time. Beebe Hall, knowing firsthand how distracted Bunny Baxley was told her she would handle the booze bash so she could concentrate on the memorial. A week before the party, Beebe Hall went over to Bunny Baxley's home to firm up the plans. Upon seeing her, Beebe Hall was shocked. Understandably, her eyes were swollen shut from crying and her skin was blotchy and red. This was from, well, there probably were many reasons, but when Beebe Hall noticed that *Fifi's* pink-jeweled dog collar was clasped around Bunny Baxley's neck, and her long red hair was pulled back with *Fifi's* barrettes, Beebe Hall was worried.

Beebe Hall poured Bunny a Southern Comfort and in the best way she could, tried to comfort Bunny Baxley. She reassured her that she and The Lawnboy had the booze bash details all finalized, and she would help with *Fifi's* memorial service plans. Bunny Baxley said, "Thanks, but no thanks. I need to do this myself, and I've already started." Bunny Baxley showed her the obituary she wrote for <u>Harper's</u> <u>Bazaar</u> and Jacqueline Susann. Beebe Hall looked at her friend and for the first time in her life, she didn't know how she was going to help her rebound. She poured her another Southern Comfort and said, "I'm here for you, just talk to me about your pain." Bunny Baxley wiped her eyes, blew her nose, looked at her friend, Beebe Hall, and said, "I thought it was her hip. You know the problem she has always had with hip dysplasia, and how she swaggered and staggered. *Fifi's* orthopedic veterinarian had reassured me it wasn't life-threatening, but when *Fifi's* autopsy report came back, and I read that the cause of death was from liver failure, not hip dysplasia, I was shocked. I would have sent her to a liver specialist if I had only known."

Bunny Baxley continued. "I knew something was wrong. I just couldn't pinpoint it. I thought *Fifi* might be heading for a breakdown because she didn't get excited and jump up and down when I splashed her with my new Jean Patou perfume. Also, she didn't seem to care when I was dressing her up in a new Coco Chanel, hand-rolled, silk scarf. Then, when her eyes started to turn yellow, and her new Jackie-O sunglasses didn't help the problem, I knew something was really wrong. I made appointments with several specialists, but she died before they could examine her."

Bunny Baxley asked her friend to make her a Margarita in *Fifi's* baccarat crystal margarita glass. She said, "It was one of her favorite drinks. Oh how she liked to lick the salt off the rim." "You know," she continued, "I never liked the salt. It made me retain fluids, but *Fifi* sure enjoyed it!"

Thank goodness Johnny Baxley came home, so Beebe Hall could leave. She had never seen her friend quite this distraught, but she knew she would have to stand beside her when The Executives' Wives' Cookbook Committee and their spouses came to the Baxley's home to sample the drinks.

Beebe Hall arrived in the afternoon and was glad to see that her friend was trying to pull it together. Bunny Baxley wore a pink, sheer number because, as she said to her friend, "that's what *Fifi* would have wanted me to wear." The house looked like a *Fifi* shrine. There were oil paintings of *Fifi* in every room and glass door cabinets filled with *Fifi* mementos. There was even a memorial guest book on the front entrance table. Beebe found one of *Fifi's* crystal dog dishes and put it by the guest book along with a lit eternal candle. She told her friend, Bunny Baxley, "The ladies will be bringing memorial cards and we need a place to put them." Bunny Baxley was touched and surprised by her friend's attention to details. Before the guests arrived, Beebe Hall had lit candles in every room and The Lawnboy and his staff had the bar well-stocked and ready to go.

[51] *When Johnny Baxley saw that his wife was having trouble 'staying vertical', he ran and got one of her favorite chairs so she could sit.*

135

When the guests arrived, the Baxleys greeted them. They had formed a two-person receiving line. [51] Most of the guests offered their condolences and gave the Baxleys big hugs. Maribelle Biche just said, "I'm sorry to hear of your loss," and immediately headed for the bar. Martha Payne just said, "I sense your pain," and her husband headed for the bar so as to spare Martha Payne from hearing ice crack. Katrina Canfield, cold and calculating as could be, didn't even mention *Fifi's* name when she said her forced 'hello'. Mrs. Elmer Steele acted like nothing had happened, and Beebe Hall overheard Doris Dupré say to Maribelle Biche, "Can you believe it, it was only a dog?" Bunny Baxley was so miffed she flicked an olive at Doris Dupré.

It took about an hour for everyone to 'liquor up'. Most of the guests commented on the wonderful drink recipes, and the touching favors. Sterling silver swizzle sticks, that were engraved with *Fifi's* name and topped with silver poodles added a nice touch.

Mrs. Elmer Steele asked Bunny Baxley if she had actually made the orange bitters. With that comment, Johnny Baxley started to boil under his collar. He gently, but firmly, took Mrs. Elmer Steele aside, and even though he wanted to throw her out of his house, he calmed down and said, "Today is not the day to be inappropriate. You see how she's suffering?" She glared at him and huffed back to the bar. She looked like a steam engine blowing black smoke.

Most of the guests toasted *Fifi* and that was of great comfort to Bunny Baxley. Everyone had their share to drink, but the mood at the party was somber so everyone left early. The Lawnboy cleaned up and informed the Baxleys that all the sterling silver swizzle sticks were gone. Bunny Baxley was too preoccupied to care.

When everyone had left, the Baxleys poured themselves stiff nightcaps and opened all the memorial cards. They were both surprised and touched at the generous amount of memorial money that was donated in honor of *Fifi*. Bunny Baxley told her husband that she was going to buy a new cocktail dress with the money, because that's what *Fifi would* have wanted her to do. [52] He agreed, and commented that in

his practice he had seen people do worse things with donated money.

Bunny Baxley waited for her husband, Johnny, to go to bed so she could, as she told him, 'have just a little alone time'. When she knew he was sound asleep, she tiptoed over to her jewelry chest and took out two, hand-cut, Baccarat, crystal glasses. With glasses in hand, she went into her very large closet. In the corner of the closet where her shoes were stored, she opened a 'secret' shoe box which held her private stash. She quietly left the room and proceeded to the wet bar with her goods. She took the shaker out of the bar cabinet, and filled it with ice, two shots of kalua, two shots of vodka and two shots of cream. In a circular, methodical way she jiggled the ingredients. As if in a trance, she poured the contents into the glasses. She paused for a moment and everything around her seemed surreal. She felt as if she were looking at the Grand Canyon and its seemingly bottomless pit for the first time.

She gazed into the mirror and adjusted her hair. She went over to her new 8-track and put on Esquivel, the recording with the barking dog. Bunny Baxley loved well-played lounge music and so did *Fifi*. She picked up the drinks, a large painting of *Fifi* and went out to her patio, lit a Pall Mall, took a drag, exhaled, picked up both drinks, raised her glasses to doggy heaven and said out loud, "This one's for you, *Fifi*. Tell your friend, *Laika*, I'm drinking a White Russian for both of you. Also tell *Lakia* that Nikita can't bury him because there's no place for a cold war in doggie heaven. Keep warm and God speed."

Postscript: Bunny Baxley passed out on the patio and slept there all night. When Johnny Baxley found her in the morning, she was 'just coming to'. He helped her in the house and he knew in his mind that his Bunny would be okay.

Cosmopolitan

1 oz. 75 proof Stolichnaya Gold-labeled vodka – or
2 oz. of 80 proof for medicinal purposes
½ oz. Cointreau

---

[52] *Mrs. Elmer Steele requested that her check go to children in distress. As Bunny Baxley said to her husband, "She knows that if anyone was in distress it was Fifi, and I know Fifi would be distressed if I didn't spend the money on a new cocktail dress. So there."*

½ oz. freshly-squeezed lime juice
½ oz. real cranberry juice
Combine the above ingredients with ice, and vigorously shake in a shaker. Pour contents into a martini glass and garnish the rim with a lime slice.

Commonly referred to as a 'cosmos' by casual people, or 'Cranberries for my Kidneys' by Bunny Baxley, this drink has always been one of Bunny Baxley's favorites because:
(1) It has the same name as her very favorite fashion magazine.
(2) She has been partial to the colors pink and red since junior high - (the time in her life when she was first introduced to Slow Gin Fizzes by her trusted friend, Beebe Hall).
(3) Her urologist, a close personal family friend who trusts Johnny Baxley to manage his money because he isn't afraid to give him a little inside information continually reminds her to drink cranberry juice every time she feels like she is coming down with a urinary tract infection. Poor dear, when those insidious infections plague Bunny Baxley, as they often do, the only comfort and relief she can find is in her Cosmopolitans.

Gin Swizzle

3 shots gin
2 ounces lime juice
2 ounces charged water
1 teaspoon sugar
1 dash bitters

Mix the gin, lime juice, charged water, sugar and bitters in a shaker with ice – (not within earshot of Martha Payne). Strain into a pretty, crystal, low ball glass filled with crushed ice. Stir with a festive, hand-blown swizzle stick.

The 'real' recipe calls for two shots of gin, but Bunny Baxley likes them strong!

Gin Fizzzzzzzzle Swizzzzzzzzy a' la Bunny

3 shots gin
squeeze of a large lemon
1 teaspoon sugar
charged water

Jiggle the gin, lemon juice and sugar with ice until the sugar is completely dissolved. Pour everything into a frosty, crystal, highball glass that is half-filled with ice. Top it off with charged water. Pretty it up with two colorful straws and your favorite swizzy swizzle stick.

If Bunny Baxley happens to have a paper cut, she skips the lemon juice and adds a little more gin.

Tom Collins

2 or 3 shots gin (depending upon your mood, and who you are serving)
1 ounce lemon juice
3 ounces charged water
1 teaspoon sugar

Mix it up and make it pretty with a couple of cherries, a thin slice of lemon and a thin slice of orange.

Bunny Baxley saves calories whenever possible. When a recipe calls for sugar, she often substitutes the sugar with saccharin.

Fuzzy Navel

1 shot peach schnapps
1 shot orange juice
1 shot triple sec

Fill a tall glass with chopped ice, pour in the peach schnapps, orange juice and triple sec. Stir with a swizzy, swizzle stick.

Bunny Baxley loves peaches and a Fuzzy Navel 'hits the spot' for her.

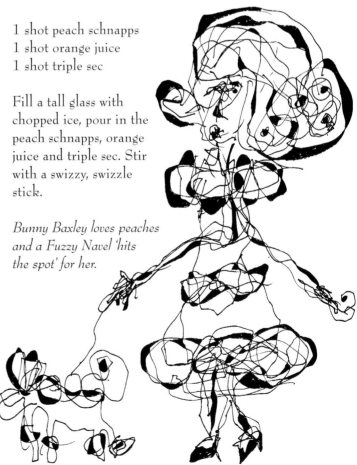

Singapore Sling

2 shots of gin
2 tablespoons cherry brandy
3 tablespoons Cointreau
1 shot grenadine
lemon juice from one lemon, squeezed
1 teaspoon sugar
3 shots charged water

Jiggle everything except the charged water and strain into a tall glass. Add the charged water. Pretty it up with a lemon twist, Chinese paper umbrella and a Maraschino cherry.

Rusty Nail

2 shots scotch whiskey
1 shot Drambuie whiskey

Pour the booze in a low ball glass over crushed ice. Stir carefully. Down it quickly before it dilutes.

Bunny Baxley likes to tell her friends they need to update their tetanus shots before they consider drinking her 'Rusty Nails.'

Old Fashioned

1 teaspoon sugar
sprinkle of bitters
2 shots bourbon

Mix the sugar and bitters into a low ball glass until it's as syrupy as Mrs. Molly McCurdle.
Add a good amount of crushed ice before you pour in the bourbon. Make it pretty with a cherry, a twist of lemon and a twist of orange. Above all, make sure a swizzy, swizzle stick is stirring things up.

Bunny Baxley once told Beebe Hall, "I think they named this drink after Mrs. Elmer Steele and Mrs. Samuel Squire.

Gin and Tonic

2 shots gin
some tonic water

Jiggle the gin with the tonic and pour it into a tall glass that is filled with ice cubes. Add a wedge of lime for looks.

Bunny Baxley calls this drink quick, easy and effective.

Sea Breeze

2 shots vodka
2 shots cranberry juice
4 ounces grapefruit juice

Pour the vodka into a pretty glass that has been filled with ice cubes. Throw in the cranberry and grapefruit juice. Garnish with a lime wedge.

Bunny Baxley says the drink should look sort of 'girly pink' if it's made right.

Piña Colada

2 shots pineapple juice
2 shots white rum
1 ½ shots coconut cream
1 teaspoon sugar

Jiggle all the ingredients with ice in a shaker and strain it into a cocktail goblet or Collins glass. Pretty it up with a slice of pineapple and a cherry.

According to 'Hoyle', a Piña Colada, properly made, should be prepared in a blender. Bunny Baxley doesn't like blenders because: (1) they're noisy which drove Fifi nuts; (2) they're noisy and they always drove her nuts; (3) there are too many parts to screw together; and (4) they take too much time to wash.

Pink Lady

2 shots gin
2 teaspoons grenadine
2 teaspoons heavy cream
1 teaspoon lemon juice
1 shot egg white

Dip the rim of a pretty champagne glass in grenadine and then roll the rim in sugar. Jiggle the gin, cream lemon juice and egg white in a shaker, and strain the mixture into the champagne glass.

While at a party, Bunny Baxley once caught Mrs. Elmer Steele licking the sugar off the rim of the glass. She nudged Beebe Hall and said, "Just look at her. The way she's going at it, you'd think she was licking S & H Green Stamps." Beebe Hall whispered back, "Maybe she needs a new hamper for her husband's 'dirty laundry.'"

B-52

1 shot Kahlua
1 shot Irish cream
1 shot Grand Marinier

Layer the drink by pouring the Kahlua over the back of a chilled teaspoon into a shot glass. Next pour in the Irish cream and finish with the Grand Marinier.

This method is too time-consuming for Bunny Baxley and some of her friends who have hand tremors. Her sure fire way is to 'shakeitallupinashaker' with a little ice and pour it in a lowball glass. Bombs Away!

Brandy Alexander

2 shots cognac
1 ½ shots *Crèam de Cacao*
1 shot heavy cream

Jiggle the cognac, *Crèam de Cacao* and cream in a shaker with ice. Strain into a low ball glass. Sprinkle a little ground nutmeg on top, and Voila!

This is Bunny Baxley's favorite after-dinner drink. The cream helps line the stomach and the warm feelings she gets from the drink makes her think of a long, lost grandma who made chocolate chip cookies. She never had a grandma like that; she just yearned for one.

Grasshopper

2 shots *Crème de Menthe*
2 shots *Crème de Cacao*
2 shots cream

Jiggle it all up and strain into a cocktail glass. *Bon Appétit!*

Bunny Baxley likes to float some green plastic grasshoppers in the glass just to watch how Martha Payne jumps upon seeing them.

Hot Toddy

2 shots brandy
1 tea bag, brewed
1 tablespoon honey
1 squirt lemon juice

Brew the tea and pour it into a coffee mug. Pour in the brandy, mix in the lemon and stir.

Bunny Baxley says this drink is better than cough syrup when it comes to treating a cold, cough or doldrums. She also knows it's a drink that evokes the same nostalgic feelings that one gets when looking at Currier and Ives pictures of horses dancing in the snow, pulling sleighs filled with bundled up people and red, silk tie robes that movie stars wear while lounging around in front of a fireplace with nothing to do but drink, and reflect on how they are going to 'get even' with all the people they dislike.

Manhattan

¾ ounce sweet vermouth
2 ½ ounces whiskey
1 dash bitters
Maraschino cherry
1 twist of orange or lime peel

Mix the vermouth, whiskey and bitters in a glass. Add the ice cubes. Garnish with a Maraschino cherry and a twist of orange or lime peel.

This was Johnny Baxley's favorite drink that Bunny served him when he came home. Of course, she has one ready for herself. Sometimes she puts a little bit of cherry juice in her drink. That's the way Fifi liked her Manhattans.

Mrs. Doris Dupre's Garden Dinner

Cocktail
WHITE RABBIT

Hors D'Oeuvres
RABBIT PÂTÉ WITH ASSORTED CRACKERS

Salad
CHIFFONADE SALAD GARNISHED WITH CHRYSANTHEMUMS

Entre
RAW CARROTS

ESCALLOPED POTATOES AUX GRATIN

SAUTÉED RABBIT GARNISHED WITH MARIGOLDS, ROSE PETALS, VIOLETS, AND NASTURTIUMS

Désert
DORIS' FRUIT AND FLOWER DÉSERT
CHOCOLATE COVERED RAISINS

140

DORIS DUPRÉ'S GARDEN DINNER PARTY

Everyone on The Executives' Wives' Cookbook Committee anticipated Doris Dupré's Garden Dinner Party with both trepidation and curiosity. They all attended because they had never been invited to her home and because most of them wanted to retrieve items that were stolen from their homes. As Mrs. Elmer Steele said to Maribelle Biche, "All roads lead to the Duprés."

A few days before Doris Dupré's party, Mrs. Elmer Steele called the members of The Executives' Wives' Cookbook Committee and said, "I think we need to band together and look out for each other's stolen goods. I put together a list of what we're missing and I have copies for everyone."

Both Katrina Canfield and Mrs. Christina Pebbleworth-Stafford told Mrs. Elmer Steele that they didn't need copies. They both told her they didn't have anything stolen, but rather they were going to return items that Doris Dupré had left at their homes. Mrs. Elmer Steele didn't know what either Katrina Canfield or Mrs. Christina Pebbleworth-Stafford meant by their statements, but she surmised after talking to them that it wasn't good. She didn't get too upset with either Katrina Canfield or Mrs. Christina Pebbleworth-Stafford's problems. She had other issues with them and just thinking about it sent her into a dither and a huff.

Doris Dupré was both dreading and looking forward to hosting The Executives' Wives' Cookbook Committee. As she said to her husband, Klog, while she was setting up 'traps' for her guests, "I'm sorry I ever agreed to join The Executives' Wives' Cookbook Committee. Except for a couple of them, they're a bunch of jealous, drunk snoops. By the time I am finished rigging up our house, they're going to 'run like rabbits', and I can't wait."

On the evening of the party, everyone arrived at about the same time. As the Steeles were driving down the *allée* and approaching the Dupré's home, Mrs. Steele said to her husband, "For crying out loud, I feel like we're pulling up to a pawn shop, rather than a party."

Doris and Klog greeted their guests, and intentionally made everyone feel like intruders. By the looks on their faces, Doris could tell everyone was utterly amazed and envious of her home, especially her gardens. Using an authoritative voice, she informed them that The Lawnboy would give a tour of the gardens. They all obediently followed The Lawnboy as if he were The Pied Piper.

While they were on the walking, garden tour, Mrs. Steele handed out the list of stolen goods she knew Doris had swindled. She said to each one of the ladies, "Pretend you're on a scavenger hunt, and if you see anything on the list, don't be afraid to shove it in your handbags." She had no sooner said this to Mrs. Michael Stellar when she spotted her missing Winston Churchill door knocker secured on the Dupré's garden shed. Mrs. Elmer Steele came prepared. She pulled a screw driver out of her handbag, unscrewed the door knocker and placed it into her handbag. Then she pulled a bottle of red nail polish out of her handbag, opened it and wrote a message that reads, "To the victor belongs the spoils; that rightfully belongs to me, you thief." She was going to write more, but she ran out of nail polish.

When the guests returned from their garden tour, Klog Dupré seated them in the dining room. As Mrs. Christina Pebbleworth-Stafford looked at the menu card, she was horrified. She said to her husband, "We're leaving. These people are so unnecessary." Mrs. Elmer Steele, who of course, was into the menu, was also horrified at the gall of the Duprés to serve not only rabbit, but food that rabbits would eat. No matter what it took, she decided she was going to fight it out until the end.

Martha Payne became so anxious at Mrs. Christina Pebbleworth-Stafford's reaction she whispered to her husband, "We have to leave or I am going to pass out." He knew she was angsted and agitated, so they followed the Pebbleworth-Staffords and left quietly. Doris Dupré was in the kitchen and grinned like the Grinch when she saw what had happened. She whispered to her husband, who was also in the kitchen, "Four down, twenty-six to go."

141

It didn't take long for the other guests to literally 'fall like dominos'. Dr. E.O. Bittleduke had excused himself from the table. When he didn't come back in a reasonable amount of time, Mrs. E.O. Bittleduke became visibly nervous, summoned The Lawnboy, whispered in his ear and right away the two of them excused themselves to go on 'another hunt'. Thank goodness, Dr. E.O. Bittleduke hadn't gotten very far. They found him sitting on a bench in the garden. Somehow he had managed to turn on all the floodlights. He was audibly talking to himself about needing more light for performing a tricky hysterectomy. Mrs. E.O. Bittleduke decided right then and there that they needed to leave. She told The Lawnboy to let the Duprés know that 'The Doctor' wasn't feeling right, that she was sorry, and they needed to leave immediately. Upon hearing the news, Doris Dupré whispered to her husband, "Six down, twenty four to go."

As Mrs. Molly McCurdle was passing the rabbit pâté to Mr. Biche, she noticed the knife on the plate was a Francis I pattern and all of a sudden it dawned on her that she was missing the same knife. She raised her hand, just like she did in first grade when she had to go to the bathroom. She said, "Doris, do you have the Francis I pattern as well?" Doris Dupré didn't respond, but got up and went to the kitchen. 'Eagle-eyed' Mrs. Elmer Steele heard the conversation and immediately asked for the rabbit pâté. When in her hand, she took the knife, wiped it off with her dinner napkin and put it in her handbag. She said to Mrs. Molly McCurdle, "There, mission accomplished." Mrs. Molly McCurdle was so upset she excused herself and left. Her husband followed. Doris Dupré, who was in the kitchen and was listening to the conversation on a recording device she had 'rigged up'. She looked at The Lawnboy who was working and said, "Eight down, twenty-two to go." He didn't understand what she meant, but she often times made bizarre comments so it didn't bother him.

Right after the McCurdle's left, Mrs. Chatterton whispered to Mrs. Bigsbee and they both excused themselves to the powder room. After they had shut the door, Mrs. Chatterton said to Mrs. Bigsbee, "For some reason I am a little unsteady on my feet. Oh, dear, it seems like I always need help." Mrs. Bigsbee, who wasn't any more steady on her feet than her

friend, paid no attention to what her dear friend, Charlotte said. However, she did notice all the lipstick samples, the ones that she had given as favors and were missing, sitting in a pretty bowl on Doris' counter. "Hey, Charlotte, remember these?" Her friend, Charlotte, looked at the samples, used one to freshen up her lipstick, winked at her friend and said, "Let's look in her medicine cabinet, maybe we can do an "'even trade.'"

When they opened the door to the medicine cabinet, ping pong balls rained like hail. Without saying a word, they both started to exit at the same time. Ping pong balls bounced in the sink, bidet and all over the floor. In their rush to leave, Mrs. Stanley Bigsbee stepped on a ping pong ball in such a way that it squirted up and hit Mrs. Charles Chatterton right between the eyes. Mrs. Charles Chatterton fell down like someone who had just been shot. Mrs. Stanley Bigsbee panicked, then her adrenaline kicked in. She grabbed Mrs. Charles Chatterton by the wrists and tried to pull her out of the powder room, like someone would pull a drowning victim out of the water and onto the shore. She just about had Mrs. Charles Chatterton in the hall, when she accidently stepped on another ping pong ball, slipped and fell on top of Mrs. Charles Chatterton in a criss-cross position. At that point they both passed out. Hearing the noise, the Squires got up from the table to see what had happened. The Lawnboy followed them. Upon seeing the ladies on the floor, Mr. Samuel Squire, said, "Interesting, they're laid out like the St. Andrew's Cross. I remember, once in England . . ." At this point, Mrs. Samuel Squire, who was so horrified at seeing the ladies and hearing what her husband said, grabbed him by the arm and escorted him out the door.

The Lawnboy went back to the dining room and called for help. Like a herd of horses on a stampede, Mr. Stanley Bigsbee, Mr. Charles Chatterton, Doris Dupré and her husband Klog Dupré ran to see what had happened. The Lawnboy pulled Mrs. Stanley Bigsbee off Mrs. Charles Chatterton and sat her up. He tried to get Mrs. Charles Chatterton to sit up, but she slumped down again. One at a time, he put the two ladies over his shoulders and carried them out to their cars. Their husbands followed and the four of them left the party. As Doris and Klog Dupré returned to the dining room, she said to him, "We killed six birds with one stone. Fourteen down, sixteen to go." Bunny and Beebe, oblivious to what was happening, were drinking one White Rabbit cocktail after another. When Klog Dupré refilled Bunny Baxley's glass for the fourth time, he put a sterling silver swizzle stick in the drink. "She looked at it and said, "I used to have some of these. I wonder what my housekeeper ever did with them." Mrs. Elmer Steele overheard what Bunny Baxley said and took action. When Bunny Baxley put her drink down and turned away, Mrs. Elmer Steele grabbed the swizzle stick and put it in her handbag. When Bunny Baxley looked back, she noticed the swizzle stick was gone and said, "*Abracadabra*, I thought I was the only one who could do magic tricks with swizzle sticks. Oh well, easy come, easy go."

Johnny Baxley, who had a 'gut feeling' that the next incident would involve his wife and Beebe Hall, announced that they needed to leave because of some urgent business. Nobody saw him on the telephone, but Jimmy Hall knew what Johnny Baxley was doing. They all left. Their wives didn't care because they were too buzzed to know what was transpiring and they were losing their attention span.

Doris Dupré was delighted. She hand-motioned to her husband, "Eighteen down, twelve to go."

Doris Dupré had The Lawnboy serve dessert which included a bowl of chocolate-covered raisins. Right away, Mrs. Grant Goldman-Hues and Mrs. Elmer Steele both spotted the rabbit-embossed spoon in the dish of raisins. When it was passed, Mrs. Elmer Steele whose handbag was filling up, put the spoon in her handbag and with a nod let Mrs. Grant Goldman-Hues know she had taken it for safe-keeping. Mrs. Grant Goldman-Hues was thankful and right after they finished dessert, she announced that they had to leave. Well-choreographed, the Stellars, the Hurlingers and the Biches all announced their imminent departures.

Doris Dupré knew she had 'won'. In her mind she calculated the kill, "Twenty-six down, four to go." As she knew would happen, she was down to the 'tough ones'. She was getting uncomfortable knowing what could transpire. Of course, her hunch was right.

At this point in the evening, the Canfields, and the Steeles both excused themselves. She knew they were up to 'no good'. Mr. Canfield went outside and Klog followed him. Mr. Canfield 'made small talk' with Klog Dupré, while his wife, Katrina Canfield , was shoving a bag full of lucky rabbit's feet in the powder room bidet and toilet. After she had finished, she put a note on top of the rabbit's feet that read, "Lucky you." She went outside. Her husband, privy to what she was doing, got the car, and they departed.

At the same time that Katrina Canfield was in the powder room, the Steeles had wandered into the artillery room. While Mr. Elmer Steele was admiring the massive amounts of rare, rabbit taxidermies in glass cases on every wall, his wife realized she was 'in luck'. Like a kid in a candy store, she spied everything she came for that was still missing. She opened her handbag and dropped Mrs. Charles Chatterton's lighter into it. She spotted Mrs. Michael Stellar's Mint Julep glass and rescued it. At this point, she noticed not only the small, rare, antique flag the Squires were missing, but a gun which Mr. Elmer Steele had been missing. "Look," she yelled to her husband, "That's your missing revolver, isn't it?" Mr. Steele was dumbstruck. While Mrs. Elmer Steele was putting the folded flag into her handbag, Mr. Elmer Steele opened the gun cabinet. Something triggered the door to slam shut. He handed the gun to his wife. She shoved it in her overflowing handbag while he desperately tried to open the door. He started to pound on the door. The pounding was so loud and desperate that The Lawnboy came to investigate. He opened the door. Upon seeing him, the Steeles hurriedly thanked him and tore out of the house with the loot in hand.

Upon watching the action from their rigged, close-circuit television set, the Dupré's high-fived each other while Doris yelled, "Thirty down, none to go."

To celebrate, they poured themselves drinks. The phone rang and Doris answered. All she heard on the other line was "*Vini, Vidi, Vici.* "She knew what had happened. She went outside, turned on her flood lights and started shooting. Hearing the shooting, The Lawnboy had all he could handle, both physically and mentally. After he cleaned up, he heard Doris Dupré shooting the rabbits in her gardens. He went into the living room, laid down on the oriental rug that he had just vacuumed and made a snow angel. He knew Doris didn't like 'tracks' left in her house, but he decided after tonight he needed to help the other ladies on The Executives' Wives' Cookbook Committee by making a statement.

Postscript: The next morning Doris had to call a plumber. The rabbit's feet had plugged up her toilet.

White Rabbit

3 ounces vodka
3 ounces vanilla liqueur
1 ⅛ ounce whole milk
1 ounce ice

Place all the ingredients in a shaker. Pour in a highball glass that has been filled with ice.

Bunny Baxley thought the White Rabbit drink tasted healthy. She said to Beebe Hall, "I bet this drink is good medicine for our tummies."

Rabbit Pâté

1¼ pounds rabbit meat
1 pound pork sausage

2 eggs
2 tablespoons sour cream
2 ounces cognac
1 teaspoon salt
½ teaspoon pepper
1 large shallot, minced
½ teaspoon garlic salt
¼ teaspoon nutmeg
2 thyme sprigs, minced
4 parsley sprigs, minced

3 bay leaves

Using a meat grinder, grind the rabbit. Add the pork sausage and blend in a blender. Place the blended meat in a bowl and add the eggs, sour cream, cognac, salt, pepper, shallot, garlic salt, ground nutmeg, thyme

and parsley. Blend well. Place the mixture in a tureen or baking dish, and place the bay leaves on top. Cover and bake at 350° for 1 ½ hours. Cool.

This can be made one day ahead and refrigerated. Before serving, cut in thin slices and put on a beautiful plate surrounded by a variety of interesting crackers and crystallized flowers.

This time, Mr. Biche asked for the recipe.

Chiffonade Salad with Chrysanthemums

1 head romaine lettuce, cut into long strips
1 head iceberg lettuce, cut into long strips
2 grapefruit, peeled and sectioned
3 green peppers, diced
2 tablespoons chives, finely chopped
2 tablespoons ripe olives, shredded

Chiffonade salad dressing

⅔ cup olive oil
⅓ cup vinegar
1 clove garlic, minced
1 teaspoon sugar
1 teaspoon salt
½ teaspoon ground pepper
½ teaspoon paprika

On individual salad plates, lay the strips of romaine lettuce in the same direction. On top of the romaine lettuce , lay the strips of iceberg lettuce in the opposite direction. On top of the lettuce, arrange grapefruit sections, diced green peppers, chives and shredded olives.

In a blender, mix the olive oil, vinegar, garlic, sugar, salt, pepper and paprika. Shake the dressing ingredients and drizzle over salads right before serving.

Mrs. Charles Chatterton ate the grapefruit out of the salad. She has been on the grapefruit diet for years. For once she found something, she could eat at a party.

Escalloped Potatoes aux Gratin

4 pounds potatoes
2 cups whole milk
2 teaspoons salt
1 clove unpeeled garlic

2 tablespoons butter

2 cups Swiss cheese, grated
2 cups cream
2 teaspoons pepper
4 tablespoons butter

Peel the potatoes and slice them into ⅛ inch thickness. Place the potatoes in a pan and cover with the milk. Add the salt and bring to a boil. Boil for approximately 15 minutes. Make sure the milk doesn't scorch. Drain.

Rub a large baking dish with the garlic clove. Brush the dish with the butter.

Pour ½ of the potato slices into the prepared baking dish. Add 1 cup Swiss cheese, 1 cup cream and 1 teaspoon pepper. Repeat the layer including the Swiss cheese, cream and pepper layers. Put 4 tablespoons of butter pats on top and bake at 350° for 30-40 minutes or until potatoes are tender, milk has been absorbed and the top is nicely browned.

Most of the ladies took a couple of bites of the potato dish. As Maribelle Biche said to Mrs. Elmer Steele, "Besides the salad, it's the only thing on the menu I can stand to eat." Mrs. Elmer Steele replied, "I'm saving room for the dessert."

Sautéed Rabbit

4 rabbits, boned
9 tablespoons butter
2 cups white wine
8 tablespoons carrots, finely chopped
6 tablespoons celery, finely diced
6 tablespoons onion, finely diced
2 bunches thyme, finely chopped

6 tablespoons dried cherries
6 tablespoons chokecherry jelly

1 teaspoon salt
1 teaspoon pepper

In a large saucepan, place rabbit, butter, white wine, carrots, celery, onions and thyme. Cover with water and bring to a boil. Reduce heat and simmer for about 40-50 minutes and the liquid has been reduced and the rabbit is browned.

Carefully add the dried cherries and the chokecherry jelly. When the jelly is melted and the cherries are puffed, the dish is ready to be served.

Put on a large platter and decorate with more red, dried cherries, marigolds, rose petals, violets and nasturtiums.

Most of the ladies on The Executives' Wives' Cookbook Committee ate meat, but certainly not rabbit meat. They all surmised that Doris Dupré killed the rabbits herself.

Doris' Fruit and Flower *Désert*

4 small packages raspberry-flavored gelatin
4 cups boiling water
4 cups cold water
¼ teaspoon raspberry liqueur

3 cups heavy cream
1 ¼ cup sugar
1 teaspoon vanilla flavoring
3 pints of raspberries

Boil the water, add the gelatin and stir until the gelatin is dissolved. Add the cold water which has been mixed with the raspberry liqueur. Chill until almost firm. Whip the cream with the sugar and vanilla. Set aside. Whip the gelatin and fold it into the whipped cream. Fold in 2 pints of fresh raspberries. Place mixture into a large rabbit mold. Refrigerate. Before serving, unmold the gelatin mixture and center it on a crystal plate. Decorate with the extra raspberries and crystallized rose petals.

Rose Petals and Violets

Doris Dupré was famous for her flower petal garnishes. Her flower petals were picked, dipped into a foamy egg white/water mixture (3 egg whites to 1 teaspoon water), and then coated in granulated sugar.

Everyone suspected that, (except for the chocolate-covered raisins and the crackers), all the ingredients came from the Dupré's garden.

Mrs. Maribelle Biche's Dinner Party

···· Cocktails ····

···· Hors d'oeuvres ····

Shrimp Cocktail
Cornucopia Canapés
Deviled Crab

···· Salad ····

Spinach Salad with Hot Bacon Dressing

···· Entre ····

Asparagus Patties
Kartoffel Glacé (German Potato Balls)
Filet Mignon with Mushroom Sauce

···· Dessert ····

Red Devil's Food Cake with Brandy Sauce
Coffee

MARIBELLE BICHE'S LAMB AND LEEKS DINNER PARTY

The 'many-mooded' Maribelle Biche was at her wits end with The Executives' Wives' Cookbook Committee recipe tasting parties. She was the last one of the group to showcase her recipes for the ladies, and she couldn't wait until it was over.

The day before her party, while she and her husband were eating dinner, she looked up at him and said, "Blah, blah, blah. I'm sick and tired of this soap opera in slow motion that has too many commercials. I should have been the president of this committee. I would have called a spade a spade and none of this nonsense would have happened. If I had been in charge, I would have kicked most of them off the committee and sent them to detox. It wouldn't have bothered me if any of their feelings were hurt, either. They don't care what's in this cookbook. In all truthfulness, most of them can't cook and certainly, none of them can cook like me."

"It's all so staged, everyone's trying to be so pretentious and they can't even do that right. It's all such a *façade*. That's what it is. You should have seen Mrs. Jonathan Hurlinger at her party. She just sat, sampled and smiled like this project was all her creation. Of course, she had to act so high and mighty because she was elected the president! Oh, la de da! Like we needed to bow down to her, and then she had the nerve to tell us that she was going to set the standards high. Oh my, she was the one who was going to raise the bar for all of us and what did she do? She hired a 'so-called' famous, French chef with no last name to cook at her party. She has no clue what it takes to master French cooking. She's pathetic. Then, she acts like the recipes are all hers and she's not at liberty to share them. What a farce."

"Then, there's Martha Payne, who's too disturbingly fearful to even boil water! Pray tell me, what's she doing on a cookbook committee anyway? Is that desperate and lonely? Mrs. Molly McCurdle serves little lolly lollipops to The Executives' Wives' Cookbook Committee. Help! Spare me from this torture! Someone should have informed her, this isn't the Girl Scouts."

"I should have known Beebe Hall's party would go up in flames and Bunny Baxley should have canceled her party instead of thinking everyone needed to sit around and mourn her sorry, dead, alcoholic poodle. Neither of those ladies have an ounce of common sense. Their brain cells are popped and pickled."

"To add insult to injury, I had to sit at a make-up demonstration at the Bigsbees. You'd think she was hosting a Stanley Party. Where was her mind? To top it all off, I've had to waste all my time and energy to raise funds for children and puppies in distress. Why? Why is it up to me to help them? I don't even like puppies and children."

Mr. Robert Biche, who as of late could hardly stand to look at his wife, much less listen to her, got up from the table, fixed himself a stiff drink and said, "I don't want to listen to you anymore. But look at it this way, lady, once this party is over, you can call it your good deed done for the year." "Now please," Maribelle Biche shot back, "I've already done my good deed for the year. Did you forget I went to your mother's funeral?"

He looked at her in disgust and said, "Just think of all the people who are privileged to be a target of your anger." "No," Maribelle calmly replied, "I don't get angry, I get even." "You've got that right, and I'm sure you can't wait," Mr. Biche snorted back. With that he walked out of the house. He couldn't take any more, even though he hated to leave the delicious dinner she had prepared.

Maribelle Biche was right. She couldn't wait to get even and like Brutus, she plotted her scheme. She had chosen and signed up to serve asparagus patties and Filet Mignon with Mushroom Sauce for her entre. She knew that nobody, outside of Mrs. Christina Pebbleworth-Stafford would remember, so she decided to confirm her suspicion and serve lamb and leeks instead.

The morning of the recipe tasting party, she had all her 'get even' plans in place. The Lawnboy, who had come early to help set up, instinctively knew she was up to something, but he had worked for her long enough to know that this was her 'normal' behavior.

She said to The Lawnboy, "Set up four tables and cover them in white linens. I want you and the other staff I've hired to serve the food plated to the tables. When you are serving, I want you to clearly understand that you are to act professionally. After you set the tables, I will personally place the name cards on the tables."

When he saw her seat the Canfields with the Paynes, the McCurdles with the Pebbleworth-Staffords, and the Squires with the Duprés, he knew she was putting people who annoyed her the most, with people who annoyed each other the most. He sensed it was the calm before the storm.

Maribelle Biche went out of her way to make everyone feel uncomfortable, even her husband. She stared each and every one of them down and waited until she could sense that they felt 'the chip on her shoulder' before she said, "Hello." She loved to watch people squirm. She had them exactly where she wanted them.

When she announced that dinner would be served, she said, "Tonight the dinner is all about the food and I cooked every bit of it." When they discovered where they were going to be seated, each and every one of them knew what she was doing, and some of them decided they were going to get even.

When Bunny saw that she had a big, old lamb chop on her plate, she said, "I'm sorry, but, ugh, I haven't been able to eat lamb since my daddy read me Mary Had a Little Lamb." Mrs. Molly McCurdle, said, "I've always felt the same way, too." Maribelle Biche ignored their comments, but was a little unnerved that they had actually stood up to her, especially Mrs. Molly McCurdle.

Mrs. Christina Pebbleworth-Stafford decided it was her turn. She said, "Excuse me, but weren't you to serve Fillet Mignon with Mushroom Sauce?" Maribelle Biche calmly looked at her and said, "Oh, really?" The rest of the ladies couldn't say anything because they couldn't remember what she had chosen to serve. Her forecast was right. Mrs. Christina Pebbleworth-Stafford, however, so annoyed that she was forced to sit with the McCurdles, decided she would continue the

banter. "By the way, Maribelle, I thought you, the superb gastronome that you are, would surely embrace the *Brillot Savorin* theory of cooking. I am puzzled why you don't embrace it in its' entirety." [53] Maribelle Biche knew what she was talking about, but nobody else had a clue. Dr. E.O. Bittleduke, who was lost in thought on how to cut his lamb chop, looked up and said, "*Brillot Savarin*, um, I think I went to med school with him. I wonder what he's up to now? Pass the ketchup."

Everyone could sense that Mrs. E.O. Bittleduke was embarrassed and horrified at her husband's response, but before she could think of some way to smooth things over, Mrs. Charles Chatterton, who at this point couldn't remember where she was, rescued Mrs. E.O. Bittleduke. She asked, "Is that the name of that fabulous French wine?" Mrs. Stanley Bigsbee, who wasn't any more coherent than her friend, chimed in, "That sounds good to me. I'll have another glass of that, too."

Mr. Biche secretly enjoyed listening to the ladies throw his wife off her course. On the other hand, he was thankful that several of the men told his wife that her lamb chops were delicious.

Everyone except Mr. and Mrs. Elmer Steele felt so uncomfortable at the Biche's home and couldn't wait to get out of there. As they were leaving, Maribelle Biche approached Doris Dupré, stood right in front of her as to block her from leaving and said, "Excuse me, but I think you have one of my knives in your purse. I caught you red-handed." Doris Dupré, horrified she had been both accused and caught, opened her purse, gave it back to Mariabelle Biche and quickly left.

While this confrontation was in progress, Mrs. Jonathan Hurlinger, tip-toed into the kitchen. She graciously thanked the Lawnboy for all he had done for all of them. She slipped him a wad of bills and said, "You helped us all through our parties and I know it wasn't always easy. We couldn't have done it without you, and more than once you saved the day." He thanked her and with a dazzling smile shared, "I've enjoyed the experiences. A smile, a thank you and a glass of lemonade go a long way."

[53] *What Mrs. Christina Pebbleworth-Stafford meant was Maribelle Biche's personality did not complete 'the pleasures of the table.'*

150

Shrimp Cocktail

30 large shrimp, boiled

1 cup chili sauce
1 cup ketchup
1 teaspoon salt
1 cup prepared horseradish
¼ tablespoon Tabasco sauce
2 tablespoons Worcestershire sauce
3 tablespoons whiskey
2 tablespoons lime juice
1 cup parsley, finely chopped

Clean shrimp by deveining and discarding the heads and shells, making sure the black line is removed from back of the shrimp. Leave the tails intact. Boil the shrimp for 3-4 minutes, or until they are opaque. Chill.

In a bowl, combine the chili sauce, ketchup, salt, horseradish, Tabasco sauce, Worcestershire sauce, whiskey, lime juice and parsley. Stir and chill.

Line a large, glass bowl with lettuce and place shrimp in it. Set the bowl in a larger, glass bowl that has been filled with ice. Allow some of the shrimp to have tails hanging over the smaller of the two bowls. Serve the cocktail sauce in a smaller version of the two other bowls and provide a small ladle for dipping the sauce.

Mrs. Jonathan Hurlinger should have known better than to taste the shrimp. She broke out in hives. It wasn't the first time this had happened to her.

Cornucopia Canapés

30 slices salami

2 pounds cream cheese, softened
½ teaspoon pepper
dash of horseradish

black olives
green stuffed olives

Roll salami slices into cornucopias. Secure with toothpicks that have colored cellophane ends. Mix the cream cheese, pepper and horseradish together. Fill each cornucopia with the cream cheese mixture. Serve on a bed of lettuce. Surround the cornucopias with black and green stuffed olives.

Bunny Baxley speared a few olives from the cornucopias display and put them in her martini.

Deviled Crab

2 pounds crab meat

8 tablespoons butter
4 tablespoons flour
1 ½ cups milk
3 teaspoons dry mustard
4 teaspoons Worcestershire sauce
dash of Tabasco sauce
4 teaspoons lemon juice
1 teaspoon salt
½ teaspoon black pepper
½ teaspoon cayenne pepper

4 tablespoons butter, melted
2 cups bread crumbs, dry

Clean and drain the crab meat. Sauté onions in butter until they are soft. Add the flour and stir. Slowly add the milk and stir until it is thick. Stir in dry mustard, Worcestershire sauce, Tabasco sauce, lemon juice, salt black pepper and cayenne pepper. Add the crabmeat and blend. Place the crab meat mixture into twelve, individual, custard cups or shells. Dot each serving with melted butter and bread crumbs. Bake at 350° until the tops are brown. Serve the deviled crab on a warmed platter. Garnish the platter with parsley sprigs and lemon wedges.

As Katrina Canfield's husband was putting some deviled crab on his plate, she whispered to him, "If a person looked up the name 'deviled crab' in the dictionary, the second meaning could be Maribelle Biche."

Spinach Salad
with Hot Bacon Dressing

2 pounds spinach, thoroughly washed and dried
⅔ cup almonds, thinly sliced and toasted

8 slices bacon, fried and chopped
4 eggs, hard boiled and chopped
2 medium red onions, thinly sliced and separated into rings

Hot bacon dressing

2 cups salad oil
1 cup red wine vinegar
2 teaspoon salt
2 teaspoons garlic salt
½ teaspoon white pepper
2 teaspoons sugar

Toss the spinach and almonds together. Place spinach/almonds on individual salad plates. Sprinkle bacon bits, hard boiled eggs and onion rings atop each salad. In a saucepan combine the salad oil, red wine vinegar, salt, garlic salt, white pepper and sugar. Bring to a boil. Just before serving, drizzle hot dressing on each salad. Serve with cloverleaf rolls or bread sticks.

Mr. Elmer Steele dripped some hot bacon grease on his flag tie. Mrs. Elmer Steele tried to be inconspicuous when she attempted to clean it with her napkin that she had dipped in her water glass. She was horrified that he didn't care, and everyone saw it. The grease stain remained.

Asparagus Patties

2 bunches asparagus, chopped
2 cups almonds

2 small onions, finely chopped
2 teaspoons salt
2 teaspoons paprika
2 teaspoons garlic powder

8 tablespoons butter

In a food grinder or blender, chop the asparagus and almonds. Remove mixture from the blender and place it in a large bowl. Combine the onions, salt, paprika and garlic powder. Mix well, and add it to the asparagus mixture. Chill. Form the asparagus mixture into patties. Melt the butter in a large skillet. Place the asparagus patties into the skillet and brown them on each side. Serve on a large platter.

This is Maribelle Biche's recipe, but she served leeks instead.

Kartoffel Glacé

8 large baking potatoes, peeled and mashed
4 tablespoons butter
2 slices bread, cubed
1 teaspoon salt
½ teaspoon nutmeg
2 eggs, well beaten

Cook potatoes, mash and cool. In a skillet melt the butter and add the cubed, bread slices. Cook until they are medium brown. Take the cooled potatoes and add the salt, nutmeg and eggs. Mix in the cubed, bread slices and form into small balls. Place the potato dumplings into a large kettle of salted, boiling water. Reduce the heat and simmer uncovered for approximately 12 to 15 minutes. The dumplings will be floating on the top when they are done. Carefully take them out of the water and put them on a tray that has been decorated with sprigs of parsley.

Bunny Baxley thought the dumplings looked like worn out tennis balls. She looked at them, turned up her nose and whispered to Beebe Hall, "Ugh, this looks like some food a person would serve people in distress."

Filet Mignon with Mushroom Sauce

8 pounds *filet mignon*
2 teaspoons salt
2 teaspoons pepper

3 teaspoons sherry
4 tablespoons lemon juice, concentrated

8 strips bacon

Salt and pepper the *filet mignon*. Marinate the *filet mignon* with sherry and lemon juice for several hours. Place bacon strips on top of the filets, securing them with toothpicks. Broil quickly at high heat for 8 minutes, then broil slowly for 3 minutes.

Mushroom sauce
¾ cup butter
3 cups mushroom, sliced

5 tablespoons flour
2 teaspoons salt
1 teaspoon pepper

½ cup white wine
¼ cup cognac

In a saucepan, melt butter and add mushrooms. While the mushrooms are cooking, slowly add the flour, salt and pepper. Simmer for 6-7 minutes. Add the whipping cream and simmer for 3 minutes. Stir in wine and cognac. Stir. Remove from heat and cover the sauce. Ladle over steaks before serving.

Maribelle Biche would have preferred to serve filet mignon rather than lamb chops, but she was glad she proved her point.

Red Devil's Food Cake with Brandy Sauce

3 squares chocolate, unsweetened

1 ½ cups cake flour, sifted
1 ¼ teaspoons baking soda
½ teaspoon salt
1 ½ cups sugar

½ cup shortening
1 cup buttermilk
2 eggs

Melt the unsweetened chocolate and set aside. In a bowl, sift together the cake flour, baking soda, salt and sugar. Add the shortening, buttermilk and eggs. Beat for 3 minutes. Add the melted chocolate and beat for another 2 minutes. Divide the batter into three 8 inch greased and floured round cake pans. Bake them for approximately 40 minutes at 350°.

Brandy Sauce

4 tablespoons butter
1 cup powdered sugar
¼ cup brandy
yolks of 2 eggs, well beaten
½ cup whipping cream
2 egg whites, stiffly beaten

1 pint whipping cream
½ cup sugar
1 teaspoon vanilla

Cream the butter and gradually add the powdered sugar. When it is blended, add the brandy. Add the egg yolks and the cream, and cook in a double boiler until it thickens. Pour this mixture over the stiffly beaten egg whites until everything is well blended. Drizzle this mixture over the cake. Cut the cake into 4 inch square pieces.

Combine the whipping cream, sugar and vanilla. Beat until the cream is thick. Place a dollop of whipped cream on each serving.

Mrs. Elmer Steele couldn't get enough of the brandy sauce. Her husband was thoroughly disgusted by the way she was eating.

PART III

THE LADIES
AND THEIR
CHARITY BALLS

MRS. JONATHAN HURLINGER

BEEBE HALL

MRS. ELMER STEELE

MRS. CHARLES CHATTERTON

MRS. STANLEY BIGSBEE

MRS. MOLLY McCURDLE

MRS. GRANT GOLDMAN-HUES

MRS. SAMUEL SQUIRE

MRS. MICHAEL STELLAR

MRS. E. O. BITTLEDUKE

KATRINA CANFIELD

MARTHA PAYNE

MRS. CHRISTINA PEBBLEWORTH-STAFFORD

BUNNY BAXLEY

DORIS DUPRÉ

MARIBELLE BICHE

THE LA LA LA LA LIPSTICK CHARITY BALL

Bunny Baxley was honored and touched when the Executives' Wives' Cookbook Committee President, Mrs. Jonathan Hurlinger, asked her to co-chair the La La La La Lipstick Ball with Mrs. Stanley Bigsbee. She had never been asked to co-chair anything; and it had been many years since Mrs. Stanley Bigsbee was entrusted to be in charge of any type of monumental undertaking.

The La La La La Lipstick Charity Ball was not only a fund raiser to raise funds for printing and publishing The Executives' Wives' Cookbook, but also a ball to honor and thank The Executives' Wives' Cookbook Committee for all their relentless hard work, caring dedication, and, of course, their vision to see worthy causes and address them.

From the beginning, Bunny Baxley and Mrs. Stanley Bigsbee took the job very seriously and met several times to brainstorm. Over many drawn-out martini luncheons, Bunny Baxley reiterated to Mrs. Stanley Bigsbee many smashing ideas that were both novel and brilliant. Like good wine aging, her ideas flowered into fruition. In her sing-song voice, she mesmerized Mrs. Stanley Bigsbee with her ideas on floral arrangements, music, favors, menus and entertainment to the point where Mrs. Stanley Bigsbee's brain couldn't soak in any more. Bunny had indeed put her in a stupor. It didn't take long for Mrs. Stanley Bigsbee to realize that Bunny Baxley was truly the 'muscle girl' behind the event, and she was the logical one to run with it. Mrs. Stanley Bigsbee knew, as co-chair, that she had to pull her weight. She graciously offered to host the La La La La Lipstick Charity Ball kick-off luncheon, in addition to choreographing the workshop on "The Art of Applying Lipstick Properly After the Main Course."

Before the kick-off luncheon took place, Bunny Baxley and Mrs. Stanley Bigsbee picked four vice presidents. They were: Mrs. Charles Chatterton, as their 1st Vice President, Beebe Hall as their 2nd Vice President, Mrs. Grant Goldman-Hues, as their 3rd Vice President, and Mrs. Jonathan Hurlinger as their 4th Vice President.[54]

They made a smart move in picking these ladies. Bunny Baxley and Mrs. Stanley Bigsbee had wonderful intentions for everything to run smoothly, but as Bunny Baxley said to Mrs. Stanley Bigsbee when she, Bunny Baxley, had forgotten to go to the first meeting, "Oh, the best laid plans of mice and men. There'll be another day." The second meeting didn't work out any better. This time Bunny Baxley was there, but Mrs. Stanley Bigsbee had fallen asleep in her Cadillac in the country club parking lot, and didn't wake up until the meeting was over. When she finally did make it into the club, everyone had left except Bunny Baxley, who was having, as she told Mrs. Stanley Bigsbee 'one more for the road.' Mrs. Stanley Bigsbee slurred something unintelligible about her new pills, and the last thing she remembered was wiping lipstick off her teeth and the steering wheel. Bunny told her not to worry because they still had one more meeting before the kick-off luncheon. At the third meeting, Mrs. Grant Goldman-Hues and Mrs. Jonathan Hurlinger told Bunny Baxley and Mrs. Stanley Bigsbee that they had met and planned out the whole ball. Bunny Baxley and Mrs. Stanley Bigsbee were relieved. Bunny Baxley grabbed her drink, hoisted it up, looked at the group and said, "I'll drink to that. Ta da!"

Postscript: The La La La La Lipstick Ball was a smashing success. The night of the ball, the ladies let down their hair and were 'smashed.'

---

[54] *They chose these ladies because they would have a good time planning the ball, and at least two of them -Mrs. Grant Goldman-Hues and Mrs. Jonathan Hurlinger -would 'take the ball' if need be.*

THE BUTTERFLY BALL

The purpose of The Butterfly Ball was three-fold: (1) to let the community know that The Executives' Wives' Cookbook Committee was serious about raising awareness and funds for children and puppies in distress; (2) to let the others, who chose not to join the committee, marvel at the committees' brilliance and importance; (3) to take a break, get dolled up, twirl, have some fun, and realize that 'all work and no play makes Jack a dull boy.'

Mrs. Michael Stellar and Mrs. E.O. Bittleduke were the 'perfect two-some' to co-chair The Butterfly Ball. They were organized, visionary and masters at executing all of the details. The only mistake they made was to ask Mrs. Molly McCurdle to help them with decorations. She, envisioning the ball as a Southern prom set in Tara with magnolia and azalea trees, had to be told The Butterfly Ball was going in a different direction. She agreed, even though she didn't understand.

Everyone on The Executives' Wives' Cookbook Committee came to The Ball. They were all bedecked, be-gowned, and be-jeweled. There were other ladies in attendance at The Butterfly Ball ladies in their social circle who had been sent an invitation by Mrs. Elmer Steele to join The Executives' Wives' Cookbook Committee, but had chosen to ignore the invitation. The Executives' Wives' Cookbook Committee knew that these ladies were envious of the attention and adoration that was bestowed upon them, and 'The Committee,' as they called themselves, were masters at flaunting it.

Postscript: All in all, everyone agreed that The Butterfly Ball was remarkable, and everyone, including Mr. Elmer Steele was on their best behavior. Mrs. E.O. Bittleduke had her daughter by her side to watch Dr. E.O. Bittleduke. She was thankful that her daughter kept 'The Doctor' in line, and in 'his cocoon.' Only once did he refer to the ball as 'The Moth Ball', and thankfully it was later in the evening when most in attendance were too inebriated to care or understand what he said.

There wasn't much time and effort devoted to talking about children and puppies in distress, because everyone was having too much fun to think about them. Mrs. Stanley Bigsbee's daughter, Elizabeth, invited The Lawnboy to be her guest at the ball. He anxiously agreed, enjoyed Elizabeth and the attention he received from all the ladies of The Executives' Wives' Cookbook Committee.

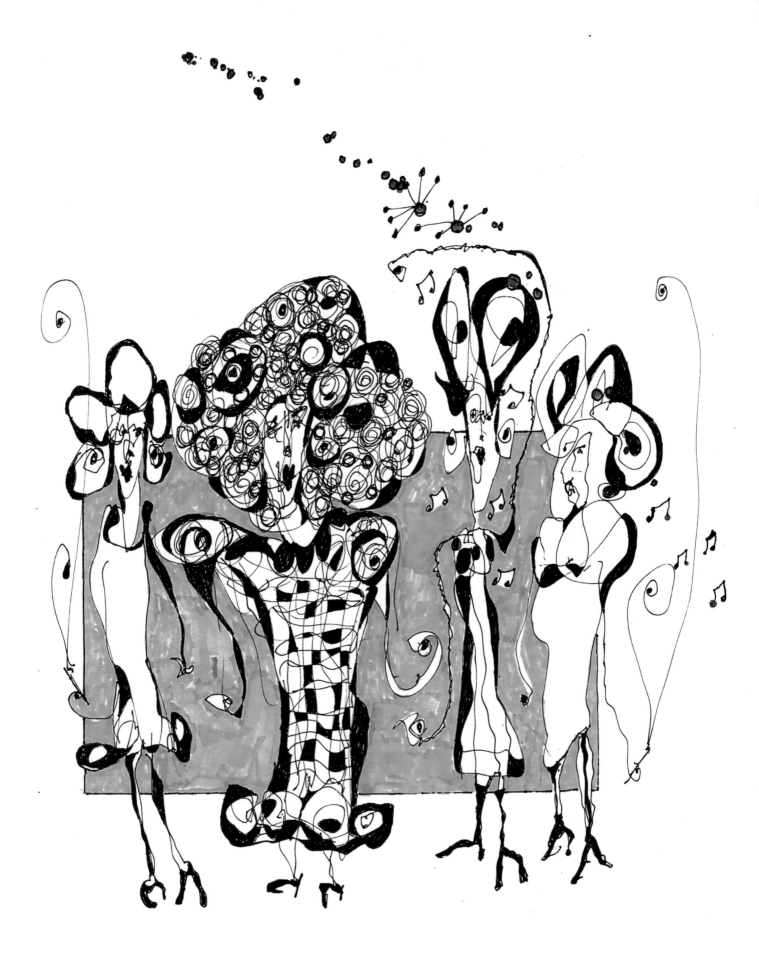

THE MASQUERADE BALL

The final ball for The Executives' Wives' Cookbook Committee was a Masquerade Ball held on Halloween. The ball was a 'thank-you' to The Ladies for all they had accomplished. It was time to play, and play they did. The costumes were original, elaborate, and told their stories. The President, Mrs. Jonathan Hurlinger, came dressed as a martini glass, surprisingly provocative, and Mr. Jonathan Hurlinger accompanied her dressed as a bottle of Beefeaters.

In character, Mrs. Stanley Bigsbee and Mrs. Charles Chatterton came dressed as mermaids. Their green shiny strapless gowns accentuated their trim figure they had worked so hard to keep, and their fishnet stockings looked great, but were full of holes by the end of the evening. Their husbands were both dressed in white sailor suits, for lack of something better to wear. As Mrs. Stanley Bigsbee said to Mrs. Charles Chatterton, "Really, it's not about them anyway. They weren't involved in all this hard work."

As was expected Mrs. Molly McCurdle came dressed as Cinderella, complete with a wand and glass slippers; and her husband, of course, was dressed as prince charming. Maribelle Biche told Mrs. Jonathan Hurlinger she thought they looked ridiculous, but that their costume choices didn't surprise anyone.

To honor her beloved dog, *Fifi*, Bunny Baxley came dressed as a poodle. She was wearing white boots up to her knees, and a short pink dress, and decorated with *Fifi's* jewels. Her husband was dressed as a fire hydrant. Beebe Hall came dressed as a cherry bomb, and her husband, Jimmy Hall, a fire fighter. It was obvious that the four of them were 'lit up' before they arrived, and nothing was going to douse the flames.

Mrs. Michael Stellar and Mrs. E.O. Bittleduke came as butterflies, complete with organza see-thru shawls that served as wings. They looked, as always, beautiful. Dr. E.O. Bittleduke came as a cocoon, and Mr. Michael Stellar was dressed as a butterfly net. They kept a low profile all evening.

Mrs. Grant Goldman-Hues, was so dazzled up in jewels, it was, as Mrs. Christina Pebbleworth-Stafford said, 'over-kill'. Her tiara, fashioned after the Platine Tiara that the pope wore, was a tad bit sacriligious, but she didn't care. It was pretty. Her husband was dressed as a chisel, and she kept his costume 'low profile' so she could shine, and shine she did!

The Pebbleworth-Staffords came dressed as Mrs. Grant Goldman-Hues told Mrs. Jonathan Hurlinger, 'the most in-your-face, look at us because we're so important costumes of the evening'. He was dressed as John Kennedy, and she, of course, dressed as Jacqueline Kennedy.

The Squires' came dressed, to no one's surprise, as George and Martha Washington. As Mrs. Stanley Bigsbee said to Mrs. Charles Chatterton, "Predictable."

Three couples came dressed true to the Halloween spirit. The Biche's were witches; Martha Payne and her husband came as sad mimes; and Katrina and Blake Canfield came as cross-dressers.

Two of the members of The Executives' Wives' Cookbook Committee came so inappropriately dressed, that even Mrs. Michael Stellar made a comment about the costumes. Doris Dupré came dressed as a hunter. To everyone's horror, she wore a real pistol in a holster buckled around her waist, and a Davy Crockett hat made from rabbit fur. If that wasn't bad enough, her husband came dressed as a dead rabbit. However, the most inappropriate costumes of the evening were worn by the Steeles. Mrs. Steele came dressed as Mary, Queen of Scots, and Mr. Elmer Steele, came in his Scottish kilt, with (as some of the ladies found out) nothing on underneath.

Most of them left the ball before they turned into pumpkins. A few of them 'twirled' until the morning, left the ball and went over to the Hall's home for a hang-over brunch.

THE EXECUTIVES' WIVES' COOKBOOK COMMITTEE

Soon after the Masquerade Ball, The Executives' Wives' Cookbook Committee met at Mrs. Jonathan Hurlinger's home to decide how they were going to sell their cookbook, and how they were going to distribute the funds that the cookbook proceeds generated.

Selling the cookbook was the easy part, because everyone, except The Duprés 'had connections.' How to distribute the funds was the hard part. Everyone had their own ideas, and it came down to Bunny Baxley's ideas, and Mrs. Elmer Steele's ideas.

Bunny Baxley, volunteered to go to animal shelters and pick up a few homeless puppies so the children in distress could play with them and realize that they weren't the only creatures in the world without homes. She said she would personally entertain both the puppies and the children by showing them all of the magic tricks she was able to do with swizzle sticks. She excitedly continued to throw out her ideas. She told them she thought The Executives' Wives' Cookbook Committee could order in some pizzas, and they should hire The Lawnboy to dish up the pizza for the children and puppies in distress. She said, "I think it would be nice if we could give everyone in distress a present so they could always remember the nice things we did for them. I was thinking we could give designer chew toys to the puppies. My *Fifi* knew the difference between an expensive chew toy and a cheap one, and expensive chew toys would be a real treat for poor puppies." Taking another drink, but hardly another breath, she continued. "I think we should give Barbie dolls to all the girls, and superman comic books to the boys. Believe me, I was an orphan, and children in distress need role models."

Mrs. Elmer Steele whispered to Mrs. Hurlinger, "Poor dear, she had awfully good intentions." Finally, Mrs. Elmer Steele, taking the bull by the horns, said it would be too hard to round up children and puppies in distress, and she thought it best that they send a check to the Animal Shelter to help the puppies, and that they should buy some books for the public library in hopes that the children in distress would check out the books and rise above their unfortunate circumstances.

Mrs. Jonathan Hurlinger thanked Bunny Baxley for all her ground-breaking ideas, but she told the group she thought that Mrs. Elmer Steele's idea might work out better, but they would have a vote on it. The vote came in 14-2 in favor of Mrs. Elmer Steele's idea. Everyone suspected that Bunny Baxley and Beebe Hall cast the dissenting votes. Mrs. Jonathan Hurlinger asked The Lawnboy to bring out another round of martinis, and after that everything was fine.

When the evening was over The Executives' Wives' Cookbook Committee officially disbanded, but the memories of their collective actions, reactions, and interactions would be forever imbedded in their minds.

They knew none of this would be possible if they didn't have the help of the strong, handsome, able-minded, hardworking person they called, The Lawnboy.

ORDER FORM

Name _____

Address _____

City_____ State_____ Zip _____

No. of copies _____ $19.95   Subtotal _____

Shipping & Handling $4.95 _____

Mn. Residents add 6.5% Sales Tax _____

TOTAL _____

Send check or money order to:

Martin House Publications PO Box 274, Hastings, MN 55033

Call (800-797-4319) or order at HYPERLINK

"http://www.scandinavianmarket.com"www.scandinavianmarket.com

Lemonade for The Lawnboy: The Executives' Wives' Cookbook Committee

is distributed by

Scandinavian Marketplace, 218 2nd Street East, Hastings, MN 55033.

Send for a free catalog and a list of other books written by Janet Letnes Martin.